Talk To Me In Korean
Workbook
Level 4

written & designed by
TalkToMeInKorean

Talk To Me In Korean Workbook (Level 4)

| 1판 1쇄 | 1st edition published | 2015. 3. 16 |
| 1판 5쇄 | 5th edition published | 2018. 7. 17 |

지은이	Written by	TalkToMeInKorean
책임편집	Edited by	선경화 Kyung-hwa Sun, 스테파니 베이츠 Stephanie Bates
디자인	Design by	선윤아 Yoona Sun
삽화	Illustration by	장성원 Sungwon Jang
녹음	Voice Recording by	선경화 Kyung-hwa Sun
펴낸곳	Published by	롱테일북스 Longtail Books
펴낸이	Publisher	이수영 Su Young Lee
편집	Copy-edited by	김보경 Florence Kim
주소	Address	04043 서울 마포구 양화로 12길 16-9(서교동) 북앤빌딩 3층 롱테일북스
		3rd Floor, Book-And Bldg. 16-9, Yanghwa-ro 12-gil, Mapo-gu, Seoul, KOREA
이메일	E-mail	TTMIK@longtailbooks.co.kr
ISBN	978-89-5605-715-6	14710

Talk To Me In Korean Workbook
Level 4

Contents

How to Use
the Talk To Me In Korean Workbook

This workbook is designed to be used in conjunction with the Talk To Me In Korean Level 4 lessons, which are available for free at TalkToMeInKorean.com. Developed by certified teachers to help you review and reinforce what you've learned in the Talk To Me In Korean lessons, this workbook contains 3 main categories of review and 13 types of exercises:

Categories

1. Vocabulary
2. Comprehension
3. Dictation

Types of Exercises

1. Checking for understanding
2. Complete the dialogue
3. Conjugation practice
4. Contraction practice
5. Dialogue
6. Expansion practice
7. Fill in the blanks

8. Matching
9. Reading
10. Spacing practice
11. Tense conjugation
12. Translation practice
13. Writing practice

The "Dictation" category is designed to aid in the development of Korean listening skills. Simply listen to the corresponding audio file and write down what you hear. In order to benefit the most from this category, it is important that you download the available audio files from www.talktomeinkorean.com/workbookaudio. These files are in MP3 format and are free of cost.

We encourage you to learn how to read and write 한글 if you do not know how to do so already. Although romanizations were provided in the Level 1 and Level 2 workbooks, starting with the Level 3 workbook, there are no romanizations. If you need help with learning 한글, we recommend that you purchase our book 한글마스터 (Hangeul Master) from MyKoreanStore.com or other major bookstores both on and offline.

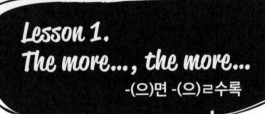
Section I – Vocabulary

Match each Korean word to its common English translation.

1. 이상하다

2. 아프다

3. 비슷하다

4. 다르다

5. 따뜻하다

6. 시원하다

7. 게으르다

8. 부지런하다

9. 쉽다

10. 어렵다

a. to be warm

b. to be difficult; to be hard

c. to be cool

d. to be weird, to be odd, to be strange

e. to be similar

f. to be easy

g. to be lazy

h. to be sick, to hurt

i. to be different

j. to be diligent; to be hard working

Section II - Comprehension

Complete the following sentences by conjugating the word provided in parentheses with -(으)ㄹ수록 and writing it in the blank, then translate each sentence to English and your preferred language (if not English).

11.   사람이 ~~~~~~~~~~~~~~~~~~~~~~ 좋아요. (많다)

   》

12.   ~~~~~~~~~~~~~~~~~~~~~~ 무서워요. (어둡다)

   》

13.   책이 ~~~~~~~~~~~~~~~~~~~~~~ 무거워요. (두껍다)

   》

14.   몸에 ~~~~~~~~~~~~~~~~~~~~~~ 맛이 없어요. (좋다)

   》

15.   ~~~~~~~~~~~~~~~~~~~~~~ 천천히 먹어야 돼요. (배고프다)

   》

16.   이 노래는 ~~~~~~~~~~~~~~~~~~~~~~ 좋네요. (듣다)

   》

Section III - Complete the Dialogue

Complete the dialogue by conjugating the most appropriate word from the box below with -(으)면 -(으)ㄹ수록.

오다	하다	크다
비싸다	재미있다	

17. A: 이렇게 비싼데, 누가 사요?

    B: 사는 사람 많아요. ＿＿＿＿＿＿＿＿＿＿＿＿ 잘 팔려요.

18. A: 비닐 봉투 큰 거 줄까요?

    B: 네. ＿＿＿＿＿＿＿＿＿＿＿＿ 좋아요.

19. A: 내일 몇 시까지 올까요?

    B: 일찍 ＿＿＿＿＿＿＿＿＿＿＿＿ 좋아요.

20. A: 이 책 빨리 읽고 저 주세요.

    B: 네. 책이 ＿＿＿＿＿＿＿＿＿＿＿＿ 빨리 읽을 수 있어요.

21. A: 한국어 공부는 잘 하고 있어요?

    B: 네. ～～～～～～～～～～～～～～～～～～ 재미있는 것 같아요.

Section IV - Dictation

Listen to the corresponding MP3 file. Repeat what you hear out loud, then write it down. Each word/phrase will be said twice.

22. Track 1:

23. Track 2:

You can download the mp3 audio files at:
www.talktomeinkorean.com/workbookaudio

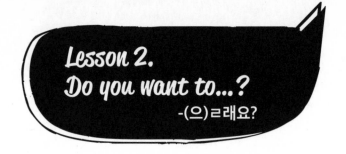

Lesson 2.
Do you want to...?
-(으)ㄹ래요?

Section I - Vocabulary

Multiple choice. Circle the best answer.

1. In Korean, 운전하다 means:

    a. to ride a bike

    b. to drive

    c. to sleep

    d. to get angry

2. Which of the following means "to [physically] follow" or "to catch up" in Korean?

    a. 들어오다

    b. 따르다

    c. 따라가다

    d. 다니다

3. 쉬다 can mean:

    a. to rest

    b. to take a break

    c. to relax

    d. all of the above

4. The word for "to postpone", "to delay", or "to put off" in Korean is:

    a. 미루다

    b. 놀다

    c. 자랑하다

    d. 미워하다

5. 결정하다 translates to:

    a. deception

    b. decision

    c. to deceive

    d. to decide

6. Which word means "to make a reservation" or "to book [in advance]" in Korean?

    a. 예약하다

    b. 예측하다

    c. 구입하다

    d. 책임지다

7. 물어보다 means:

    a. to hit

    b. to be dumped

    c. to bite

    d. to ask

8. What does 배달하다 mean?

    a. to be full

    b. to deliver

    c. to see someone off

    d. to develop

9. What is 옮기다 in English?

    a. to walk

    b. to lift

    c. to pull

    d. to move

10. How do you say "to chew" in Korean?

    a. 씻다

    b. 씩다

    c. 씹다

    d. 씸다

Section II - Comprehension

True/False - Decide if the statement is true or false. If it is false, correct the underlined term or statement so that the sentence is true.

11. The -(으)ㄹ래요 ending is usually used only in <u>formal settings</u>.

    »

12. "혼자 할게요" <u>sounds much nicer than</u> "혼자 할래요".

    ≫

13. "저는 안 갈래요" and "저는 안 가고 싶어요" both mean "I don't want to go",
but <u>"저는 안 갈래요" can mean "if you really insist, I might go"</u>.

    ≫

14. <u>You cannot put a question mark</u> at the end of -(으)ㄹ래요.

    ≫

15. If you ask a person what he/she wants by using the ending "-고 싶어요?"
in Korean, <u>it is unnatural and sounds a bit like a textbook</u>.

    ≫

Section III - Translation Practice
Translate the sentences to Korean using -(으)ㄹ래요.

16. I want to go home. =

17. I want to do it alone. =

18. I want to get some rest. =

19. I don't want to see this movie. =

20. I don't want to eat. =

21. I want to drive. =

Section IV - Dictation
Listen to the corresponding MP3 file. Repeat what you hear
out loud, then write it down. Each word/phrase will be said
twice.

22. Track 3:

23. Track 4:

Section I - Vocabulary

Use the words from the Word Bank to correctly label each picture.

Word Bank

환자   선생님   아빠   의사   손님   학생   팬   가수   직원   엄마

1.

2.

3.

4.

5.

Section II - Comprehension

Multiple choice. Circle the best answer.

6. "내일이 일요일일 리가 없어요." means:

    a. It's possible that tomorrow is Sunday.

    b. There's no way that tomorrow is Sunday.

    c. Tomorrow can be Sunday.

    d. There is no Sunday.

7. How do you say "그럴 리가 없어요!" in English?

    a. It can't be!

    b. It can't be so!

    c. That's impossible!

    d. All of the above

8. In "그럴 리가 없어요!", what word is conjugated with -(으)ㄹ 리가 없어요?

    a. 그렇다

    b. 그렇다

    c. 그래다

    d. 그러다

9. How do you conjugate "춥다" and "-(으)ㄹ 리가 없어요"?

    a. 추을 리가 없어요.

    b. 춥을 리가 없어요.

    c. 추울 리가 없어요.

    d. 추월 리가 없어요.

10. In Korean, how do you say "It's impossible that he/she doesn't know"?

    a. 알 리가 없어요.

    b. 알 수 없어요.

    c. 모를 리가 없어요.

    d. 모르 리가 없어요.

Section III- Conjugation Practice

Based on the given English translation, translate each sentence to Korean by conjugating the sentence endings provided in parenthesis and -(으)ㄹ 리가 없어요. There is no need to directly translate "he/she".

Example :
There's no way that he/she does. (-아/어/여요)
= 할 리가 없어요.

11. There's no way that he/she is going to do. (-(으)ㄹ 거예요)

=

12. There's no way that he/she is doing it (now). (-고 있어요)

=

13. There's no way that he/she did. (-았/었/였어요)

=

14. There's no way that he/she can do it. (-(으)ㄹ 수 있어요)

=

15. There's no way that he/she wants to do. (-고 싶어요)

    =

16. There's no way that he/she will do it for me. (-아/어/여 줘요)

    =

17. There's no way that he/she has to do it. (-아/어/여야 돼요)

    =

Section IV - Dictation

Listen to the corresponding MP3 file. Repeat what you hear out loud, then write it down. Each word/phrase will be said twice.

18. Track 5

19. Track 6

Lesson 4
verb ending -지(요)

Section I - Vocabulary

Define/translate each word to English using what you know or a dictionary, then write it in your preferred language (if not English).

1. 밟다 _____

2. 읽다 _____

3. 끌다 _____

4. 빌다 _____

5. 자르다 _____

6. 믿다 _____

7. 묶다 _____

8. 싸우다 _____

9. 움직이다 _____

10. 씻다 _____

Section II - Comprehension

Short answer. Please respond to the following questions in English, then write the answer in your preferred language (if not English) to help you remember more efficiently!

11. List the 2 main situations when you use the -지(요) ending:

   a.

   b.

12. List the 3 situations when you use the -지(요) ending as an interrogative (question) ending:

   c.

   d.

   e.

13. Among the five situations on the previous page, in which cases do you always speak in 반말?

   »

Section III - Conjugation Practice
Change the ending of the sentences to -지(요).

14. 우유는 거기 없어요. ↣

15. 석진 씨가 거기 갈 리가 없어요. ↣

16. 사무실이 너무 어두운 것 같아요? ↣

17. 이것은 제가 들 수 있어요. ↣

18. 그 비디오 봤어요. ↣

19. 일 끝나고 바로 집에 갈 거예요? ↣

Talk To Me In Korean Workbook

20. 이거 효진 씨가 다 해야 돼요? ↪

21. 저도 지드래곤 콘서트 가고 싶어요. ↪

Section IV – Dictation

Listen to the corresponding MP3 file. Repeat what you hear out loud, then write it down. Each word/phrase will be said twice.

22. Track 7

23. Track 8

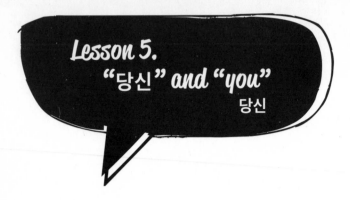

Lesson 5.
"당신" and "you"
당신

Section I - Vocabulary

Using the kinship terms from the Word Bank, complete the family tree according to how it would apply directly to you.

— Word Bank —

이모부	사촌 누나	남동생
외삼촌	아빠(아버지)	사촌 형
언니	형	엄마(어머니)
할아버지	여동생	고모
외할머니	사촌 오빠	사촌 언니
큰엄마(큰어머니)	할머니	오빠
이모	외할아버지	사촌 동생
	큰아빠(큰아버지)	

1. ～～～～ 2. ～～～～   3. ～～～～ 4. ～～～～

5. ～～～～ 6. ～～～～ 7. ～～～～ 8. ～～～～ 9. ～～～～ 10. ～～～～ 11. ～～～～ 12. ～～～～

(남자, 50세)   (여자, 48세)   (남자, 44세)

13. ～～～～ 14. ～～～～

(남자, 25세)   (여자, 23세)

15. ～～～～

(1세)

16. ～～～～   or   나 (14세)   17. ～～～～

(남자, 18세)   (여자, 9세)

Section II - Comprehension

Please respond to the following questions in English, then write the answer in your preferred language (if not English) to help you remember more efficiently!

18. How do you say "you" in Korean if you are speaking in 반말?

      »

19. How do you say "you" in Korean if you are speaking in 존댓말?

      »

20. List the 5 main situations when people use the word 당신:

    a.

    b.

    c.

    d.

    e.

Section III - Dictation

Listen to the corresponding MP3 file. Repeat what you hear out loud, then write it down. Each word/phrase will be said twice.

21. Track 9:

22. Track 10:

Lesson 6.
Word builder 3 동(動)

Section I - Vocabulary

Please define/translate each word to English using what you know or a dictionary, then write it in your preferred language (if not English).

1. 운동(運動): _____

2. 동작(動作): _____

3. 작동(作動): _____

4. 활동(活動): _____

5. 동사(動詞): _____

6. 동물(動物): _____

7. 연동(聯動): _____

8. 행동(行動): _____

9. 동영상(動映像): _____

10. 동맥(動脈): _____

Section II - Comprehension
Multiple choice. Circle the best answer.

11. What does 동(動) mean?

    a. learning, studying

    b. room

    c. movement, move

    d. frame; machine

12. In 운동(運動), what does 운(運) mean?

    a. to make

    b. to flow

    c. to connect

    d. to transport

13. Choose ONE word that best fills in the blanks.

    온라인 (   ) / 음악 (   ) / TV (   )

    a. 동작(動作)   b. 활동(活動)   c. 동사(動詞)   d. 작동(作動)

14. Choose ONE word that best completes the sentences.

A: 블로그랑 페이스북 어떻게 (   )해요?

B: 아직 (   ) 안 되어 있어요? 아주 쉬워요.

    a. 동물(動物)   *c.* 행동(行動)

    b. 연동(聯動)   *d.* 동맥(動脈)

15. Choose ONE word that best fills in the blanks.

이 (   )을 따라하세요.　/　손(   )　/　발(   )

    a. 동작(動作)   *c.* 동맥(動脈)

    b. 동사(動詞)   *d.* 연동(聯動)

Section III - Dictation

Listen to the corresponding MP3 file. Repeat what you hear out loud, then write it down. Each word/phrase will be said twice.

16. Track 11

17. Track 12

Lesson 7.
It's okay. I'm okay.
괜찮아요.

Section I - Comprehension

Multiple choice. Circle the best answer.

1. 괜찮아요 does NOT mean:

    a. Don't worry.

    b. I am okay.

    c. Everything is fine.

    d. Thank you.

2. Although it is spelled 괜찮아요, which of the following represents the correct pronunciation?

    a. 괜차하요   c. 괜차나요

    b. 괜차아요   d. 괜창아요

3. If you say "이 영화 진짜 괜찮아요," what does 괜찮아요 mean in this context?

    a. good   c. funny

    b. bad   d. not so good

4. How do you say "괜찮아요" in the past tense?

    a. 괜찮았요.   c. 괜찮았어요.

    b. 괜찮았아요.   d. 괜찮었어요.

5. How do you say "괜찮아요" in the future tense?

      a. 괜찮알 거예요.   *c.* 괜찰 거예요.

      b. 괜찮을 거예요.   *d.* 괜찬흘 거예요.

Section II - Conjugation Practice

Conjugate 괜찮다 with the given ending.

6. 괜찮다 + -지요. =

7. 괜찮다 + -(으)ㄹ 리가 없어요. =

8. 괜찮다 + -(으)ㄹ까요? =

9. 괜찮다 + -(으)ㄴ 것 같아요. =

10. 괜찮다 + -네요. =

11. 괜찮다 + -(으)ㄹ 수도 있어요. =

12. 괜찮다 + -기 전에 =

13. 괜찮다 + -아/어/여도 =

14. 괜찮다 + -(으)ㄴ데 =

15. 괜찮다 + -아/어/여서 =

Section III - Dictation

Listen to the corresponding MP3 file. Repeat what you hear out loud, then write it down. Each word/phrase will be said twice.

16. Track 13

17. Track 14

Lesson 8.
It is okay to ...,
You don't have to ...

-아/어/여도 돼요,
안 -아/어/여도 돼요

Section I - Vocabulary

Match each Korean word to its common English translation.

1. 테니스를 치다

    a. to throw away garbage/rubbish

2. 사진을 찍다

    b. to cut one's nails

3. 차를 마시다

    c. to boil water

4. 물을 끓이다

    d. to drink tea

5. 손톱을 깎다

    e. to take pictures

6. 길을 건너다

    f. to take an exam

7. 문자를 보내다

    g. to make plans

8. 계획을 세우다

    h. to send text messages

9. 쓰레기를 버리다

    i. to play tennis

10. 시험을 보다

    j. to cross the street

Section II - Comprehension
Multiple choice. Circle the best answer.

11. 되다 translates to English as:

    a. to be helpful

    b. can understand, to make sense

    c. to be worried

    d. to function; to be possible

12. -도 is used to represent the meaning of:

    a. also, too

    b. and, with

    c. about, around

    d. without

13. Which conjunction means the same thing as the verb ending -아/어/여도?

    a. 그렇지만

    b. 그런데

    c. 그러면

    d. 그래도

14. -아/어/여도 되다 means:

    a. to go (somewhere) in order to...

    b. it is okay to..., it is okay even if you...

    c. to plan to...

    d. it seems like...

15. If you add 안 in front of -아/어/여도 되다, what does it mean?

    a. you shouldn't..., you're not supposed to...

    b. don't have to..., it is not necessary to...

    c. you must not...

    d. no matter how much...

Section III - Conjugation Practice

Change the sentence to a negative AND question form, then translate each sentence to English and your preferred language (if not English).

    Example :

    지금 가도 돼요. = You can leave now.

    (negative) 지금 안 가도 돼요. = You don't have to leave now.

    (question) 지금 가도 돼요? = Can I leave now?

16. 불 켜도 돼요. = You can turn the light on.

(negative) ～～～～～～～～～～～～～～～～～～～～～～～～～～～～～～

(question) ～～～～～～～～～～～～～～～～～～～～～～～～～～～～～～

17. 내일 해도 돼요. = It's okay if you do it tomorrow; You can just do it tomorrow.

(negative) ～～～～～～～～～～～～～～～～～～～～～～～

(question) ～～～～～～～～～～～～～～～～～～～～～～～

18. 시작해도 돼요. = You can start.

(negative) ～～～～～～～～～～～～～～～～～～～～～～～

(question) ～～～～～～～～～～～～～～～～～～～～～～～

19. 이 케이크 먹어도 돼요. = You can eat this cake.

(negative) ～～～～～～～～～～～～～～～～～～～～～～～

(question) ～～～～～～～～～～～～～～～～～～～～～～～

20. 이 컴퓨터 써도 돼요. = You can use this computer.

(negative) ～～～～～～～～～～～～～～～～～～～～～～～

(question) ～～～～～～～～～～～～～～～～～～～～～～～

Talk To Me In Korean Workbook

21. 오늘 쉬어도 돼요. = You can take a day off today.

(negative) ~~~~~~

(question) ~~~~~~

Section IV - Dictation

Listen to the corresponding MP3 file. Repeat what you hear out loud, then write it down. Each word/phrase will be said twice.

22. Track 15

23. Track 16

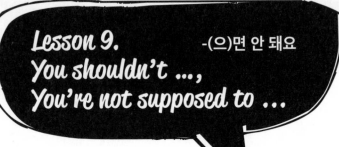

Lesson 9.
You shouldn't ...,
You're not supposed to ...

-(으)면 안 돼요

Section I - Vocabulary

Fill in each quadrant based on the given vocabulary word.

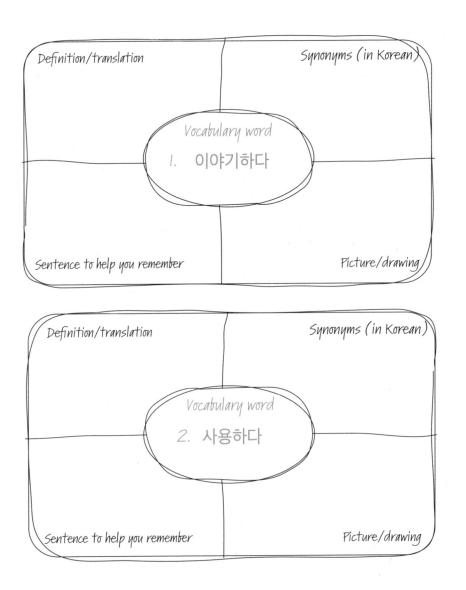

Definition/translation

Synonyms (in Korean)

Vocabulary word

1. 이야기하다

Sentence to help you remember

Picture/drawing

Definition/translation

Synonyms (in Korean)

Vocabulary word

2. 사용하다

Sentence to help you remember

Picture/drawing

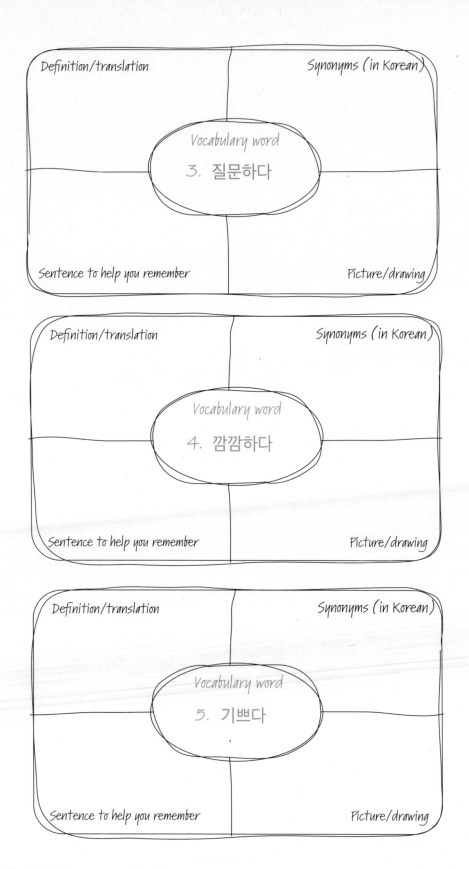

Definition/translation · Synonyms (in Korean)

Vocabulary word
3. 질문하다

Sentence to help you remember · Picture/drawing

Definition/translation · Synonyms (in Korean)

Vocabulary word
4. 깜깜하다

Sentence to help you remember · Picture/drawing

Definition/translation · Synonyms (in Korean)

Vocabulary word
5. 기쁘다

Sentence to help you remember · Picture/drawing

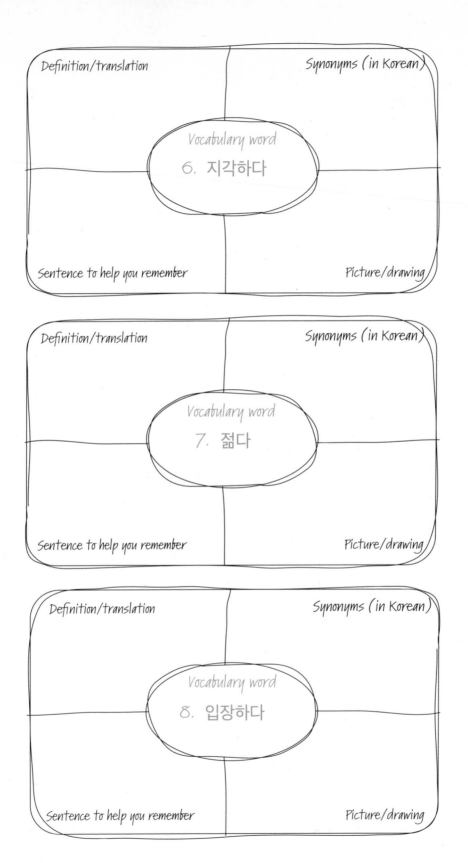

Definition/translation

Synonyms (in Korean)

Vocabulary word

6. 지각하다

Sentence to help you remember

Picture/drawing

Definition/translation

Synonyms (in Korean)

Vocabulary word

7. 젊다

Sentence to help you remember

Picture/drawing

Definition/translation

Synonyms (in Korean)

Vocabulary word

8. 입장하다

Sentence to help you remember

Picture/drawing

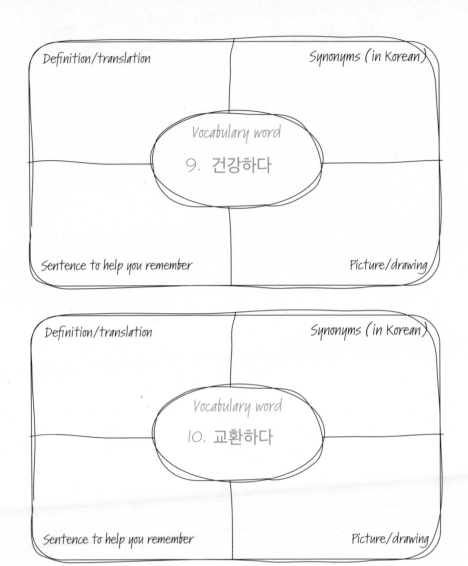

Definition/translation	Synonyms (in Korean)

Vocabulary word

9. 건강하다

Sentence to help you remember	Picture/drawing

Definition/translation	Synonyms (in Korean)

Vocabulary word

10. 교환하다

Sentence to help you remember	Picture/drawing

Section II - Comprehension

Write two opposing answers for each question.

Example :

Q: 지금 입장해도 돼요?

A: (Yes) 네. 지금 입장해도 돼요.

A: (No) 아니요. 지금 입장하면 안 돼요.

11.   Q: 이거 제가 가져가도 돼요?

A: (Yes) ～～～～～～～～～～～～～～～～～～～～～～～～～

A: (No) ～～～～～～～～～～～～～～～～～～～～～～～～～

12.   Q: 다른 채널로 돌려도 돼요?

A: (Yes) ～～～～～～～～～～～～～～～～～～～～～～～～～

A: (No) ～～～～～～～～～～～～～～～～～～～～～～～～～

13.   Q: 이거 사용해도 돼요?

A: (Yes) ～～～～～～～～～～～～～～～～～～～～～～～～～

A: (No) ～～～～～～～～～～～～～～～～～～～～～～～～～

14.   Q: 이 슬리퍼 신어도 돼요?

A: (Yes) ～～～～～～～～～～～～～～～～～～～～～～～～～

A: (No) ～～～～～～～～～～～～～～～～～～～～～～～～～

15.   Q: 다른 사람들한테 이야기해도 돼요?

A: (Yes) ～～～～～～～～～～～～～～～～～～～～～～～～～

A: (No) ～～～～～～～～～～～～～～～～～～～～～～～～～

16. Q: 사진 찍어도 돼요?

A: (Yes) ～～～～～～～～～～～～～～～～～～～～～～～～～～

A: (No) ～～～～～～～～～～～～～～～～～～～～～～～～～～

Section III - Translation Practice

Translate each sentence to Korean using -(으)면 안 돼요.

17. Am I not supposed to sell (something) here?

=

18. Am I not supposed to touch this?

=

19. Am I not supposed to go outside?

=

20. Am I not supposed to open the window?

=

21. Am I not supposed to throw this away?

=

22. Am I not supposed to get off here?

=

23. Am I not supposed to ask a question?

=

Section IV - Dictation
Listen to the corresponding MP3 file. Repeat what you hear out loud, then write it down. Each word/phrase will be said twice.

24. Track 17

25. Track 18

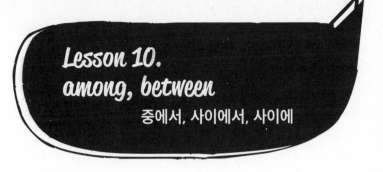

Lesson 10.
among, between
중에서, 사이에서, 사이에

Section I - Vocabulary

Using words from the Word Bank, write the name of each business in Korean below.

Word Bank

학교   약국   경찰서   은행   치과

주유소   편의점   백화점   신발 가게   우체국

1. ~~~~~   2. ~~~~~   3. ~~~~~   4. ~~~~~   5. ~~~~~

6. ~~~~~   7. ~~~~~   8. ~~~~~   9. ~~~~~   10. ~~~~~

Section II - Writing Practice

Write a sentence based on the drawing in Section I with the provided word. Use 사이에 in your sentence just as in the example.

Example : 약국은 백화점하고 편의점 사이에 있어요.

11. 편의점은 _____

12. 경찰서는 _____

13. 은행은 _____

14. 학교는 _____

15. 우체국은 _____

Section III - Comprehension

Fill in the blank with one of the following: 중에서/사이에서/사이에. Translate each sentence to English and your preferred language (if not English).

16. 요즘은 여섯 시에서 일곱 시 (   ) 해가 떠요.

    =

17. 이 가수는 한국인들 (   ) 인기가 많아요.

    =

18. 책 (   ) 있어서 안 보였어요.

   =

19. 이 세 개 (   ) 고르세요.

   =

20. 민혁 씨, 여자들 (   ) 뭐 하세요?

   =

21. 이 (   ) 먹고 싶은 것 있어요?

   =

22. 토요일하고 일요일 (   ) 언제가 좋아요?

   =

Section IV - Dictation

Listen to the corresponding MP3 file. Repeat what you hear out loud, then write it down. Each word/phrase will be said twice.

23. Track 19:

24. Track 20:

Lesson 11.
any (Part 1) 아무

Section I - Vocabulary

Please define/translate each word to English using what you know or a dictionary, then write it in your preferred language (if not English).

1. 아무나 _____

2. 아무거나 _____

3. 아무데나 _____

4. 아무도 _____

5. 아무것도 _____

6. 아무데도 _____

Section II - Fill in the Blank

Fill in the blank using one of the words in Section I. Each word is used once.

7. (   ) 좋아요. = Any place is good.

8. (　　　　　) 만지지 마세요. = Don't touch anything.

9. (　　　　　) 주세요. = Just give me anything.

10. (　　　　　) 안 갈 거예요. = I'm not going anywhere.

11. (　　　　　) 없어요? = Nobody's here?

12. (　　　　　) 올 수 있어요. = Anyone can come.

Section III - Comprehension

Circle the correct word. If both answers are possible, underline both words.

13. (아무나) (아무도) 참여할 수 있어요?

14. (아무나) (아무도) 갔다 오세요.

15. 저는 (아무거나) (아무것도) 몰라요.

16. 아직 (아무나) (아무도) 안 왔어요.

17. (아무데나) (아무데도) 가고 싶지 않아요.

18. 사람이 (아무데나) (아무데도) 없어요.

19. (아무거나) (아무것도) 시켜도 돼요?

20. (아무데나) (아무데도) 앉을 수 없어요.

Section IV - Dictation
Listen to the corresponding MP3 file. Repeat what you hear out loud, then write it down. Each word/phrase will be said twice.

21. Track 21

22. Track 22

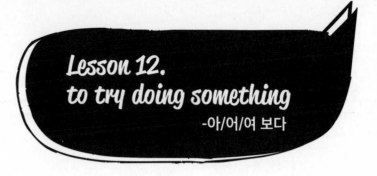

Lesson 12.
to try doing something
-아/어/여 보다

Section I - Vocabulary

Unscramble the Korean word and write it in the provided boxes to match the English definition.

1. to solve/resolve a problem:

   다를풀문제 ➤ ☐☐☐ ☐☐

2. to raise one's head:

   개를고들다 ➤ ☐☐☐ ☐☐

3. to learn Korean :

   한배우를국어다 ➤ ☐☐☐☐ ☐☐☐

4. to go into a shop:

   게에다들가가어 ➤ ☐☐☐ ☐☐☐☐

5. to start exercising:

   시하작운을동다 ➤ ☐☐☐ ☐☐☐☐

6. *to send an email:*

보다내메일이을 ➤ ☐☐☐☐ ☐☐☐

7. *to open a box:*

다열를자상 ➤ ☐☐☐ ☐☐

8. *to turn on one's cell phone:*

폰다켜드핸을 ➤ ☐☐☐☐ ☐☐

9. *to look into a mirror:*

울보다거을 ➤ ☐☐☐ ☐☐

10. *to open a window:*

문열창다을 ➤ ☐☐☐ ☐☐

Section II - Translation Practice

Translate the sentences that tell someone to try or attempt doing something by using the phrases from Section I and -아/어/여 보다.

11. Try raising your head.

   =

12. Try learning Korean.

   =

13. Try to start working out.

    =

14. Try looking into the mirror.

    =

15. Try opening the window.

    =

Using the phrases from Section 1 and –아/어/여 보다, translate the following questions to Korean.

16. Have you tried solving the problem?

    =

17. Have you tried going into a shop?

    =

18. Have you tried sending an email?

    =

19. Have you tried opening the box?

    =

20. Have you tried turning on the cell phone?

    =

Section III - Conjugation Practice

Using the sentence ending -아/어/여 보고 싶어요, write a sentence which in-cludes the given words.

Example :
파리, 가다 ➜ 파리에 가 보고 싶어요.

21. 한국, 가다 ➜

22. 마카롱, 먹다 ➜

23. 새로운 메뉴, 먹다 ➜

24. 번지점프, 하다 ➜

25. 새로 나온 카메라, 사용하다 ➜

26. 그 노래, 듣다 ➜

27. 현우 씨, 만나다 ➜

28. 경화 씨, 이야기하다 ➜

29. 중국어, 배우다 ➜

30. 새로운 일, 도전하다 ✈

Section IV - Dictation

Listen to the corresponding MP3 file. Repeat what you hear
out loud, then write it down. Each word/phrase will be said
twice.

31. Track 23

32. Track 24

Section I - Vocabulary, Part 1

Please define/translate each word to English using what you know or a dictionary, then write it in your preferred language (if not English).

1.   불안(不安) _____

2.   불편(不便) _____

3.   불만(不滿) _____

4.   부당(不當) _____

5.   불평(不平) _____

6.   불신(不信) _____

7.   불참(不參) _____

8.   불행(不幸) _____

9.   불법(不法) _____

Section II - Vocabulary, Part 2

Decide whether to use 불 or 부 to fill in each blank, then translate the words to English and your preferred language (if not English).

10. __ 주의(不注意) _____

11. __ 완전(不完全) _____

12. __ 균형(不均衡) _____

13. __ 도덕(不道德) _____

14. __ 합격(不合格) _____

15. __ 정확(不正確) _____

16. __ 이익(不利益) _____

17. __ 평등(不平等) _____

18. __ 적절(不適切) _____

19. __ 전승(不戰勝) _____

Section III - Dictation

Listen to the corresponding MP3 file. Repeat what you hear out loud, then write it down. Each word/phrase will be said twice.

20. Track 25

21. Track 26

Section I - Vocabulary

Define/translate each word to English using what you know or a dictionary, then write it in your preferred language (if not English).

1. 가끔 _____

2. 자주 _____

3. 항상 _____

4. 맨날 _____

5. 별로 _____

6. 전혀 _____

7. 거의 _____

Section II - Checking for Understanding

Place a checkmark in the box to indicate the frequency at which you do each of the listed activities.

	맨날/항상	자주	가끔	별로	전혀
8. 서점에 가다					
9. 커피를 마시다					
10. 영화를 보다					
11. 콘서트에 가다					
12. 드라마를 보다					
13. 지하철을 타다					
14. 야구를 하다					
15. 피아노를 치다					
16. 케이크를 만들다					

Section III - Reading Comprehension

Read the following passage and answer the questions.

> 나는 가끔 산에 가. 엄마는 산을 안 좋아하셔서, 항상 아빠랑 같이 가. 내가 아빠랑 자주 가는 산은 집 앞에 있는 청계산이야. 청계산은 집에서 정말 가까워서, 걸어서 갈 수 있어. 그리고 많이 높지 않아서 정상까지 쉽게 올라갈 수 있어. 서울에는 산이 참 많은데, 다른 산은 별로 안 가 봤어. 앞으로는 다른 산에도 가 보고 싶어.

17. How often does the writer go to the mountains?

    a. never

    b. sometimes

    c. seldom

    d. often

18. Which of the following has the same meaning as the underlined sentence?

    a. I am able to walk now.

    b. I can go there anytime.

    c. I can go there by myself.

    d. It is within walking distance.

19. What level of politeness is the writer using?

    a. 존댓말

    b. 반말

    c. 평말

    d. 캐주얼말

20. Which of the following statements is true about the writer?

  a. He/She always goes hiking with his/her mom.

  b. He/She has not been to many different mountains.

  c. He/She is not interested in trying out other mountains yet.

  d. His/Her mom likes mountains.

21. Which of the following statements is incorrect information about 청계산?

  a. It is a mountain.

  b. It is in Seoul.

  c. It is a high mountain.

  d. It is in front of the writer's house.

Section IV - Dictation

Listen to the corresponding MP3 file. Repeat what you hear out loud, then write it down. Each word/phrase will be said twice.

22. Track 27

23. Track 28

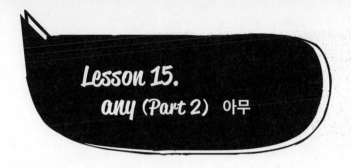

Lesson 15.
any (Part 2) 아무

Section I - Vocabulary

Use the words from the Word Bank to correctly label the feeling or emotion of each picture.

Word Bank

기분이 좋다   졸리다   놀라다   슬프다

화나다   심심하다   기분이 나쁘다   힘들다

1. ~~~~~~~~~~

2. ~~~~~~~~~~

3. ~~~~~~~~~~

4. ~~~~~~~~~~

5. ~~~~~~~~~~

6. ~~~~~~~~~~

7. ~~~~~~~~~~

8. ~~~~~~~~~~

Section II - Comprehension

9. Which of the following does NOT fit in the blank?

(   ) 말 안 했어요.

a. 아무

b. 아무한테도

c. 아무렇게나

d. 아무렇지도

10. Which of the following CANNOT be used to complete the sentence?

(   ) 전화하지 마세요.

a. 아무 말도

b. 아무 때나

c. 아무한테도

d. 아무렇지도 않게

11. Which of the following can be used in the blank?

(   ) 주지 말고 혼자 먹어요.

a. 아무 말도

b. 아무한테도

c. 아무렇지도

d. 아무런

12. Which of the following best fills in the blank?

저는 (   ) 않아요.

a. 아무 때나

b. 아무한테도

c. 아무 이야기도

d. 아무렇지도

13. Which of the following DOES NOT complete the sentence?

아직 (   ) 연락이 없어요.

a. 아무런

b. 아무렇지도

c. 아무한테도

d. 아무

Section III - Writing
Fill in the blank with one of the following words. Each word is used only once.

소식 / 일 / 약속 / 냄새 / 느낌 / 옷 / 연락

14. 아직 아무(   )도 못 받았어요.

15. 잘 지냈어요? 그동안 아무 (   )없었죠?

16. 토요일인데 아무 (   )도 없어요.

17. 저는 아무 (   )도 못 들었어요.

18. 마취를 해서 아무 (   )도 안 났어요.

19. 아무 (   ) 이나 입고 나오세요.

20. 코가 막혀서 아무 (   )도 맡을 수 없어요.

Section IV - Dictation

Listen to the corresponding MP3 file. Repeat what you hear out loud, then write it down. Each word/phrase will be said twice.

21. Track 29

22. Track 30

Lesson 16.
Spacing in Korean (Part 1)
띄어쓰기

Section I - Vocabulary

Fill in the chart. Each Korean term is a casual expression or term used in everyday Korean conversations.

Common Korean term	Common English translation
1.	Earphone
아이고	2.
3.	Cell phone
4.	Are you serious?! / Really?
5.	Awesome! / Wow! / Impressive!
파이팅/화이팅!	6.
짱!	7.
8.	Are you crazy?!
9.	OMG/ Oh my word!
셀카	10.
11.	"Best face" / Good-looking
야! (rude)	12.

Section II - Spacing Practice

Correct the spacing of each phrase.

Ex) 좋은날씨 ➤ 좋은 날씨

13. 가까운역 ➤

14. 비싼지갑 ➤

15. 추운겨울 ➤

16. 조용한방 ➤

17. 즐거운토요일 ➤

18. 부지런한사람 ➤

19. 좋은아이디어 ➤

20. 수영잘하는사람 ➤

21. 피자주문한사람 ➤

22. 아침에마시는커피 ➤

Correct the spacing of each sentence.

Ex) 책몇권샀어요? ➤ 책 몇 권 샀어요?

23. 도서관자주가요? ➤

24. 빨리말하세요. ➤

25. 조용히걸으세요. ➤

26. 어제친구만났어요. ➤

27. 숙제다하고왔어요. ➤

28. 이것은어디있었어요? ➤

29. 청소하고공부했어요. ➤

30. 저는가끔서점에가요. ➤

31. 제가그것을만들었어요. ➤

32. 저는중국어를배우고있어요. ➤

Section III - Dictation

Listen to the corresponding MP3 file. Repeat what you hear out loud, then write it down. Each word/phrase will be said twice.

33. Track 31

34. Track 32

Talk To Me In Korean Workbook

Lesson 17.
축약형 (Part 1) - 주격 조사
Word Contractions
- Topic/Subject marker

Section I - Vocabulary

Match each Korean word or phrase to its common English translation.

1. 벽지   a. computer

2. 변기   b. bed

3. 에어컨   c. washing machine

4. 전등   d. desk

5. 거실   e. wallpaper

6. 보일러   f. television

7. 식기세척기   g. air conditioner

8. 세탁기   h. remote control

9. 텔레비전   i. boiler

10. 컴퓨터   j. living room

11. 리모콘   k. toilet

12. 책상   l. dishwasher

13. 침대   m. light, lamp

Section II - Contraction Practice

Shorten the underlined part of each sentence.

Ex) <u>저는</u> 괜찮아요. ➤ 전 괜찮아요.

14. <u>나는</u> 거실에 있을게. ➤

15. <u>이것이</u> 마음에 들어요. ➤

16. <u>서울에는</u> 사람이 너무 많아요. ➤

17. <u>어제는</u> 보일러가 고장 났는데, 오늘은 세탁기가 고장 났어요. ➤

18. <u>집에는</u> 지금 누가 있어요? ➤

Expand the underlined part of each sentence.

Ex) <u>넌</u> 언제 왔어? ➤ 너는 언제 왔어?

19. <u>저게</u> 뭐예요? ➤

20. <u>그건</u> 식기세척기예요. ➤

21. <u>회사엔</u> 컴퓨터가 몇 대 있어요? ➤

22. 바다엔 언제 갔다 왔어요? ⟶

23. 여긴 에어컨이 없네요. ⟶

Section III - Dictation

Listen to the corresponding MP3 file. Repeat what you hear out loud, then write it down. Each word/phrase will be said twice.

24. Track 33

25. Track 34

Lesson 18.
the most 제일, 가장

Section I - Vocabulary

Fill in the chart. An example has been provided.

	Adjective	Meaning	제일/가장 + Adjective	New Meaning
1.	차갑다	to be cold	제일/가장 차갑다	to be the coldest
2.	밝다			
3.	멀다			
4.	뜨겁다			
5.	재미있다			
6.	얇다			
7.	가깝다			
8.	두껍다			
9.	재미없다			
10.	어둡다			

Section II - Conjugation Practice

Using the given words, create an adjective phrase in Korean. An example has been provided.

Ex) 제일, 예쁘다, 여자 ↣ 제일 예쁜 여자

11. 제일, 차갑다, 아이스크림 ↣

12. 가장, 밝다, 방 ↣

13. 가장, 멀다, 집 ↣

14. 제일, 뜨겁다, 물 ↣

15. 가장, 재미있다, 프로그램 ↣

16. 제일, 얇다, 옷 ↣

17. 가장, 가깝다, 동네 ↣

18. 가장, 두껍다, 책 ↣

19. 제일, 재미없다, 영화 ↣

20. 제일, 어둡다, 색깔 ↣

Section III - Writing Practice

Using the following given words, compose a statement or question in 존댓말. After writing each sentence, translate it to your preferred language (answers provided in English only).

Example:

〔그것, 밝다, 가장, 별〕 그것이 가장 밝은 별이에요.

= It is the brightest star.

21. 〔이것, 문제, 쉽다, 가장〕 _____

   =

22. 〔원피스, 어떤, 제일, 예쁘다〕 _____

   =

23. 〔김태희, 예쁘다, 제일, 배우〕 _____

   =

24. 〔화장실, 어디, 가장, 가깝다〕 _____

   =

25. 〔이 햄버거, 햄버거, 맛있다, 가장〕 _____

   =

Section IV - Dictation

Listen to the corresponding MP3 file. Repeat what you hear out loud, then write it down. Each word/phrase will be said twice.

26. Track 35

27. Track 36

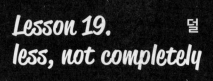

Section I - Vocabulary

Fill in the chart. An example has been provided.

Adjective	Meaning	Present tense statement using 덜	Meaning
1. 달다	to be sweet/sugary	덜 달아요.	It's less sweet/sugary.
2. 쓰다			
3. 맵다			
4. 싱겁다			
5. 느끼하다			
6. 시다			
7. 짜다			

Section II - Writing

Write one sentence using 보다 덜, one sentence using 제일/가장, and one sentence using 보다 더 (from Level 2, Lesson 21) to make a comparison between the three items in each picture. (The answers that are provided in the back are just examples of the many ways you can write a sentence.)

소요산   킬리만자로 산   에베레스트 산

8.   보다 덜: 킬리만자로 산이
_____

9.   제일/가장: _____

10. 보다 더: 킬리만자로 산이
_____

빨간색   녹색   파란색
₩5,000   ₩305,000   ₩15,000

11. 보다 덜: 파란색 가방이 _____

12. 제일/가장: _____

13. 보다 더: 파란색 가방이 _____

크리스
187cm

시우민
173cm

카이
182cm

오세훈
181cm

14. 보다 덜: 카이가 _____

15. 제일/가장: _____

16. 보다 더: 오세훈이 _____

Talk To Me In Korean Workbook

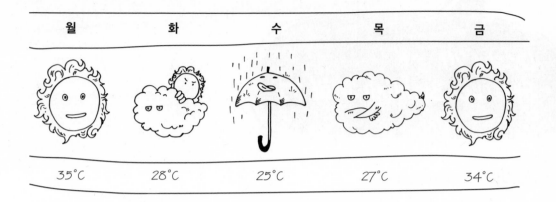

월	화	수	목	금
35°C	28°C	25°C	27°C	34°C

17. 보다 덜: 목요일이 화요일

_____

18. 제일/가장: 월요일이

_____

19. 보다 더: 금요일이 화요일

_____

Section III - Dictation

Listen to the corresponding MP3 file. Repeat what you hear out loud, then write it down. Each word/phrase will be said twice.

20. Track 37

21. Track 38

Section I - Matching

Take the sentence fragment from the A Column, match it with the most appropriate fragment from column B, and write it as one sentence on the line below.

A B

1. 결혼식을 위해서 오늘부터   한번 가 보세요.

2. 어제부터 오늘까지   다이어트 시작해요.

3. 주말에 시간이 있으면   많은 일들이 있었어요.

1. _____

2. _____

3. _____

	A	B
4.	언제부터	시험 기간이에요.
5.	지난 주부터 다음 주까지	가까운 곳으로 가세요.
6.	시간이 조금밖에 없으면	기다렸어요?

4. _____

5. _____

6. _____

	A	B
7.	밥 먹고	열심히 공부할 거예요.
8.	내일부터	눈이 많이 내릴 거예요.
9.	지금 밖에 나가면	커피 마실래요?

7. _____

8. _____

9. _____

	A		B
10.	내일도		열심히 연습할 거예요.
11.	석진 씨는		어쩌면 비가 내릴지도 몰라요.
12.	실수하지 않기 위해서		어떤 거 마실래요?

10. _____

11. _____

12. _____

Section II - Expansion practice

Complete each sentence based on what you have learned in this lesson. Answers will vary.

13. 오늘부터 한국어를 ~~~~~~~~~~~~~~~~~~~~~~~~~~~~~~~~~~~~

14. 아마 내일부터 일요일까지 ~~~~~~~~~~~~~~~~~~~~~~~~~~~~

15. 내일 시간이 있으면, ~~~~~~~~~~~~~~~~~~~~~~~~~~~~~~~~~

16. ~~_____~~ 눈이 그칠 거예요.

17. ~~_____~~ 어디에서 마실래요?

18. ~~_____~~ 한국어로 말할 거예요.

Section III - Dictation

Listen to the corresponding MP3 file. Repeat what you hear out loud, then write it down. Each word/phrase will be said twice.

19. Track 39

20. Track 40

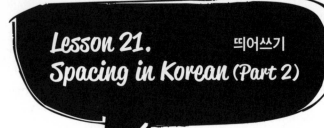

Lesson 21.
Spacing in Korean (Part 2)

띄어쓰기

Section I - Vocabulary, Part 1

Match each Korean word or phrase to its common English translation.

1. 돌려 주다

2. 돌려주다

3. 돌아 가다

4. 돌아가다

5. 빌려 주다

6. 빌려주다

a. to lend something to someone

b. to detour;
to go around the long way

c. to turn something for someone

d. to return something;
to give something back

e. to return; to go back to some place

f. to borrow something
(from someone else) for someone

Section II - Vocabulary, Part 2

Match each English phrase to its common Korean translation with the correct spacing.

7. to recognize something/someone

8. to come outside

9. to go outside

10. to come inside

11. to go inside

a. 들어 가다

b. 나오다

c. 알아 보다

d. 나 가다

e. 들어오다

f. 나 오다

g. 들어가다

h. 알아보다

i. 나가다

j. 들어 오다

Section III - Spacing

Correct the spacing of each sentence.

12. 열쇠돌려주세요. ⟶

= Please give me back the key.

13. 언제돌아갈거예요? ➤

= When will you go back?

14. 돈좀빌려줄수있어요? ➤

= Can you lend me some money?

15. 한눈에알아봤어요. ➤

= I recognized it at once.

16. 들어오세요. ➤

= Please come inside.

17. 앤디씨는밖에나갔어요. ➤

= Andy went outside.

Section IV - Dictation

Listen to the corresponding MP3 file. Repeat what you hear out loud, then write it down. Each word/phrase will be said twice.

18. Track 41

19. Track 42

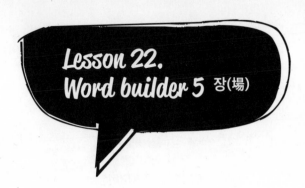

Section I - Vocabulary

Define/translate each word to English using what you know or a dictionary, then write it in your preferred language (if not English).

1. 장소(場所) _____

2. 운동장(運動場) _____

3. 주차장(駐車場) _____

4. 장면(場面) _____

5. 시장(市場) _____

6. 목장(牧場) _____

7. 수영장(水泳場) _____

8. 예식장(禮式場) _____

9. 자기장(磁氣場) _____

10. 중력장(重力場) _____

Section II - Comprehension

Multiple choice. Circle the best answer.

11. What does 장(場) mean?

    a. learning, studying

    b. room

    c. place, location, yard

    d. frame, machine

12. Based on the meaning of the word 장(場), what is the most accurate English translation of "골프장"?

    a. golf room

    b. golf frame

    c. golf study

    d. golf yard

13. 실습 + 장 = _____

    a. kitchen

    b. living room

    c. fraternity house

    d. practice room

14. The Korean word for "banquet hall" is:

    a. 예식장

    b. 연습장

    c. 연회장

d. 주방장

15. Based on the meaning of the word 장(場), what is the most accurate English translation of "공장"?

    a. factory
    b. bean place
    c. ball park
    d. office building

Section III - Dictation

Listen to the corresponding MP3 file. Repeat what you hear out loud, then write it down. Each word/phrase will be said twice.

16. Track 43

17. Track 44

Lesson 23.
Word Contractions (Part 2)
축약형

Section I - Vocabulary

Create a Korean sentence by matching the phrase on the left with the most appropriate verb on the right and write it on the line below. Choose the most accurate English translation from the "Translation Bank" and write it next to the Korean phrase. The first one has been done for you.

Translation Bank

to look for a job/position

to move to a new workplace

to fit into a job

to work, to be in paid employment

to come back from work

to quit a job

to be dismissed/fired from one's job

to get a job

직장을

1. 얻다

2. 다니다/나가다

3. 쫓겨나다/해고되다

직장에서

4. 구하다

5. 적응하다

6. 돌아오다

직장에

7. 옮기다

8. 그만두다

1.   직장을 얻다 = to get a job _____

2.   _____

3. _____

4. _____

5. _____

6. _____

7. _____

8. _____

Section II - Conjugation Practice

Fill in the blanks by conjugating one of the following: 이렇다/그렇다/저렇다.

9. ☐☐☐ = like this, in this way

10. ☐☐☐ = like that, in such a way

11. ☐☐☐ = like that (over there)

12. ☐☐☐ ☐☐ = if you do it like this

13. □□□ □□ = if you do it in such a way

14. □□□ □□ = if you do it like that

Section III - Comprehension

Re-write each sentence of the dialogue by shortening the parts which can be shortened.

15. A: 좋은 직장을 얻기 위해서는 어떻게 해야 될까요?

    ≫

    B: 그렇다면 좋은 직장은 어떤 직장이에요?

    ≫

16. A: 그렇게 하면 직장에서 해고될 거예요.

    ≫

    B: 그러면 어떡하지요?

    ≫

17. A: 보세요. 면접에서 저렇게 하면 직장을 쉽게 구할 수 있어요.

    ≫

    B: 면접이 다 저렇다면 저는 자신 있어요.

    ≫

Section IV - Dictation

Listen to the corresponding MP3 file. Repeat what you hear out loud, then write it down. Each word/phrase will be said twice.

18. Track 45

19. Track 46

Lesson 24.
훨씬
much (more), much (less)

Section I - Vocabulary

Choose the adjective from the Word Bank which best describes each picture.
Each word is only used once.

Word Bank

| 불편하다 | 길다 | 많다 | 더럽다 | 짧다 |
| 적다 | 편하다 | 강하다 | 깨끗하다 | 약하다 |

1.

2.

3.

4.

5.

6.

7.

8.

9.

10.

Section II - Fill in the Blank

Using the words in parenthesis + 훨씬 더, fill in the blank for each sentence.
Translate each sentence to English and/or your preferred language (transla-
tions in answer key are given in English.)

11. (약하다, -(으)ㄴ 것 같아요)

이 선풍기는 거실에 있는 선풍기보다 바람이 (   ).

=

12. (길다, -았/었/였어요)

영화가 생각보다 (   ).

=

13. (많다, -아/어/여요)

영화관에는 사람이 주말에 (   ).

=

14. (적다, -아/어/여요)

제 용돈은 언니 용돈보다 (   ).

=

15. (강하다, -(으)ㄴ 것 같아요)

지난해 챔피언이 (   ).

=

Using the words in parenthesis + 훨씬 덜, fill in the blank for each sentence.
Translate each sentence to English and/or your preferred language (transla-
tions in answer key are given in English.)

16. (불편하다, -아/어/여요)

오른쪽에 있는 의자가 높아도 (   ).

=

17. (더럽다, -네요)

지난번보다 방이 (   ).

=

18. (깨끗하다, -아/어/여요)

이 유리컵이 저 컵보다 (   ).

=

19. (짧다, -아/어/여서)

이 치마가 (   ) 보기 좋아요.

=

20. (편하다, -(으)ㄴ 것 같아요)

이 신발이 저 신발보다 (   ).

=

Section III - Dictation

Listen to the corresponding MP3 file. Repeat what you hear out loud, then write it down. Each word/phrase will be said twice.

21. Track 47

22. Track 48

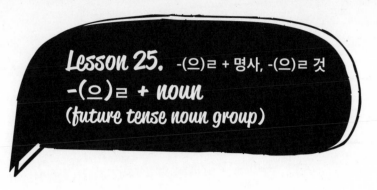

Lesson 25. -(으)ㄹ + 명사, -(으)ㄹ 것
-(으)ㄹ + noun
(future tense noun group)

Section I - Vocabulary

Create a Korean sentence by matching the phrase on the left with the most appropriate verb on the right and write it on the line below. Choose the most accurate English translation from the "Translation Bank" and write it next to the Korean phrase. The first one has been done for you.

사진을	
1. 작다	to edit a photo
2. 지우다/삭제하다	to print a photo
3. 잘 나오다	a photo is small
4. 올리다	to take a photo
5. 저장하다	a photo comes out good
6. 편집하다	to delete a photo
7. 흐리게 나오다	to save a photo
사진이	
8. 찍다	a photo comes out blurry
9. 인화하다	to transfer/load a photo
10. 옮기다	to upload a photo

1. <u>사진이 작다 = a photo is small</u>

2. _____

3. _____

4. _____

5. _____

6. _____

7. _____

8. _____

9. _____

10. _____

Section II - Conjugation Practice

Conjugate the verb and -(으)ㄹ, then add the noun as in the example. Translate the phrase to English and your preferred language (if not English).

Ex) 마시다 + -(으)ㄹ + 물 = 마실 물 / water to drink

11. 읽다 + -(으)ㄹ + 책 =

12. 초대하다 + -(으)ㄹ + 사람 =

13. 보내다 + -(으)ㄹ + 편지 =

14. 하다 + -(으)ㄹ + 일 =

15. 입다 + -(으)ㄹ + 옷 =

16. 보다 + -(으)ㄹ + 영화 =

17. 외우다 + -(으)ㄹ + 단어 =

18. 공부하다 + -(으)ㄹ + 언어 =

19. 이야기하다 + -(으)ㄹ + 사람 =

20. 쓰다 + -(으)ㄹ + 돈 =

Section III - Dictation

Listen to the corresponding MP3 file. Repeat what you hear out loud, then write it down. Each word/phrase will be said twice.

21. Track 49

22. Track 50

Lesson 26. -(으)ㄴ + 명사, -(으)ㄴ 것
-(으)ㄴ + noun
(past tense noun group)

Section I - Vocabulary

Create a Korean sentence by matching the phrase on the left with the most appropriate verb on the right and write it on the line below. Choose the most accurate English translation from the "Translation Bank" and write it next to the Korean phrase. The first one has been done for you.

		Translation Bank
	1. 물어보다	to make time for
	2. 지키다	time passes/goes by
	3. 멈추다	to spend time
시간을	4. 쏟다	it takes time
	5. 걸리다	to be punctual
	6. 내다	to have no time
	7. 다 되다	to invest/devote time
시간이	8. 쓰다	time stops
	9. 지나다/흐르다	time is up
	10. 없다	to ask the time

1. 시간을 물어보다 = *to ask the time*
    _____

2. _____

3. _____

4. _____

5. _____

6. _____

7. _____

8. _____

9. _____

10. _____

Section II - Comprehension

Translate the following phrases to Korean.

11. the movie that (someone) saw yesterday

= ☐☐ ☐ ☐☐

12. the cafe that a friend talked about

= ☐☐☐ ☐☐ ☐☐

13. the people who came here yesterday

= ☐☐ ☐☐ ☐ ☐☐☐

14. the person who came first

= ☐☐ ☐☐ ☐ ☐☐

15. the present that (someone) received from a friend

= ☐☐☐☐ ☐☐ ☐☐

Section III - Dialogue

Write a short answer in Korean to each question after reading the given dialogue.

석율: 이 책 읽어 볼래요?

그래: 네. 그런데 지난번에 빌려준 책 아직 덜 읽었어요. 요즘 책 읽을 시간이 없어서요.

석율: 괜찮아요. 두 책 다 천천히 읽고 아무 때나 주세요.

그래: 고마워요. 잘 읽을게요.

16. How many books does 그래 have to return to 석율?

17. Why hasn't 그래 finished reading the book yet?

18. When does 그래 need to return books to 석율?

Section IV - Dictation

Listen to the corresponding MP3 file. Repeat what you hear out loud, then write it down. Each word/phrase will be said twice.

19. Track 51

20. Track 52

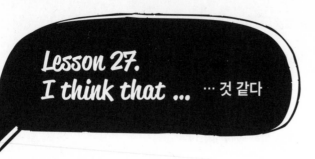

Lesson 27.
I think that ... ···것 같다

Section I - Vocabulary

Create a Korean sentence by matching the phrase on the left with the most appropriate verb on the right and write it on the line below. Choose the most accurate English translation from the "Translation Bank" and write it next to the Korean phrase. The first one has been done for you.

Translation Bank

	to calculate money
	to pay money
	to lose money
	to not have money
	to be short on money
	to have a lot of money, to be rich
	to count money
	to take out money
	to find money / to withdraw money
	to put money in something

돈을

1. 많다
2. 찾다
3. 부족하다
4. 계산하다
5. 꺼내다
6. 넣다
7. 내다

돈이

8. 세다
9. 없다
10. 잃어버리다

1. 돈이 많다 = to have a lot of money, to be rich
   _____

2. _____

3. _____

4. _____

5. _____

6. _____

7. _____

8. _____

9. _____

10. _____

Section II - Tense Conjugation

Conjugate the present tense sentence into past tense and future tense. An example has been provided.

Example :

[Present tense] 지금 하는 것 같아요.

[Past tense] **>>** 벌써 한 것 같아요.

[Future tense] **>>** 내일 할 것 같아요.

II.

[Present tense] 지금 비 오는 것 같아요.

[Past tense] **>>** 새벽에 ＿＿＿＿＿＿＿＿＿＿＿＿＿.

[Future tense] **>>** 내일 ＿＿＿＿＿＿＿＿＿＿＿＿＿.

12.

[Present tense] 길이 많이 막히는 것 같아요.

[Past tense] **>>** 길이 많이 ＿＿＿＿＿＿＿＿＿＿＿.

[Future tense] **>>** 지금 가면 길이 많이 ＿＿＿＿＿＿＿＿＿.

13.

[Present tense] 사람들이 지금 나오는 것 같아요.

[Past tense] **>>** 사람들이 다 ＿＿＿＿＿＿＿＿＿＿.

[Future tense] **>>** 사람들이 이제 ＿＿＿＿＿＿＿＿＿＿.

14.

[Present tense] 수업은 매일 10시에 시작하는 것 같아요.

[Past tense] ›› 수업 이미 ~~~~~~~~~~~~~~~~~~~~~~~~~~~ .

[Future tense] ›› 수업은 10분 후에 ~~~~~~~~~~~~~~~~~~~~~~~ .

15.

[Present tense] 현우 씨는 평소에 잠을 많이 자는 것 같아요.

[Past tense] ›› 현우 씨가 어제 잠을 많이 ~~~~~~~~~~~~~~~~~~~~~ .

[Future tense] ›› 현우 씨가 오늘 피곤해서 잠을 일찍 ~~~~~~~~~~~ .

Section III - Comprehension
Change the Korean sentences to make it sound less direct by using " ... 것 같아요".

Example :
내일 비 올 거예요. ➝ 내일 비 올 것 같아요.

16. 이거 뭐예요? ➝

17. 누가 했어요? ➝

18. 이게 더 좋아요. ➝

19. 곧 도착할 거예요. ➜

20. 저 사람 한국 사람이에요. ➜

21. 그렇게 말하면 기분 나쁠 거예요. ➜

22. 제 친구가 현우 씨랑 같이 사진 찍었어요. ➜

Section IV - Dictation
Listen to the corresponding MP3 file. Repeat what you hear out loud, then write it down. Each word/phrase will be said twice.

23. Track 53

24. Track 54

Lesson 28. -아/어/여지다
to become + adjective

Section I - Vocabulary

Choose the adjective from the Word Bank which best describes each picture.

───── **Word Bank** ─────

얕다	딱딱하다	가볍다	부드럽다
무겁다	깊다	가늘다	느리다
굵다	빠르다		

1. ~~~~~~~~~~~~~~~~   2. ~~~~~~~~~~~~~~~~

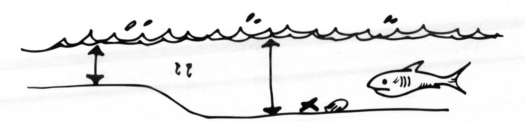

3. ~~~~~~~~~~~~~~~~   4. ~~~~~~~~~~~~~~~~

5. ～～～～～～～～～～～～

6. ～～～～～～～～～～～～

7. ～～～～～～～～～～～～

8. ～～～～～～～～～～～～

9. ～～～～～～～～～～～～

10. ～～～～～～～～～～～～

Section II - Conjugation Practice

Compose a sentence by using the word 훨씬 and conjugating the adjective with -아/어/여지다. Translate each sentence to English and your preferred language (if not English).

Example: (피부, 부드럽다) 피부가 훨씬 부드러워졌어요.
= My skin has become much softer.

11. (가방, 가볍다)

=

12. (물, 깊다)

=

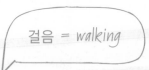

걸음 = walking

13. (걸음, 빠르다)

=

14. (다리, 굵다)

=

15. (허리, 가늘다)

=

16. (손바닥, 딱딱하다)

=

Section III - Writing Comprehension

Complete the sentence with the words provided in parenthesis by conjugating them with -(으)ㄹ수록 and -아/어/여지다, then translate each sentence to English and your preferred language (if not English).

Example: (하다, 피곤하다) 일은 많이 할수록 피곤해져요.
= The harder you work, the more tired you become.

17. (일어나다, 짧다) 늦게 ＿＿＿＿＿＿＿ 하루가 ＿＿＿＿＿＿＿.

=

18. (가다, 예쁘다) 경은 씨는 ＿＿＿＿＿＿＿ ＿＿＿＿＿＿＿ 것 같아요.

=

19. (길다, 지루하다) 동영상은 ＿＿＿＿＿＿＿ ＿＿＿＿＿＿＿.

=

20. (생각하다, 좋다) 그 사람을 ＿＿＿＿＿＿＿ 기분이 ＿＿＿＿＿＿＿.

=

21. (웃다, 행복하다) 많이 〰〰〰〰〰〰〰 〰〰〰〰〰〰〰.

=

22. (듣다, 우울하다) 이 음악은 〰〰〰〰〰〰〰 〰〰〰〰〰〰〰.

=

Section IV - Dictation
Listen to the corresponding MP3 file. Repeat what you hear out loud, then write it down. Each word/phrase will be said twice.

23. Track 55

24. Track 56

Section I - Vocabulary

Match each Korean word or phrase to its common English translation.

1. 다치다

2. 드시다

3. 벌다

4. 아끼다

5. 당첨되다

6. 지원하다

7. 사귀다

8. 약하다

9. 연습하다

10. 시작하다

a. to apply

b. to be weak

c. to get hurt

d. to start

e. to earn

f. to eat [honorific]

g. to practice

h. to get close to

i. to save

j. to win (a prize)

Section II - Conjugation Practice

The following combinations are commonly used in Korean conversation. Complete the sentence using the combination and the words provided in parenthesis. An example has been provided.

-아/어/여서 -게 됐어요. = Since I [verb], I ended up doing [verb].

Example : (다치다, 못 하다)

다쳐서 운동을 못 하게 됐어요.

11. (약하다, 시작하다)

몸이 ꞏꞏꞏꞏꞏꞏꞏꞏꞏꞏꞏꞏꞏꞏꞏꞏꞏꞏꞏꞏꞏ 운동을 ꞏꞏꞏꞏꞏꞏꞏꞏꞏꞏꞏꞏꞏꞏꞏꞏꞏꞏꞏꞏꞏꞏꞏꞏꞏꞏꞏꞏꞏꞏꞏꞏꞏ.

12. (당첨되다, 가다)

이벤트에 ꞏꞏꞏꞏꞏꞏꞏꞏꞏꞏꞏꞏꞏꞏꞏꞏꞏ 콘서트에 ꞏꞏꞏꞏꞏꞏꞏꞏꞏꞏꞏꞏꞏꞏꞏꞏꞏꞏꞏꞏꞏꞏꞏꞏꞏꞏꞏ.

13. (옮기다, 가다)

직장을 ꞏꞏꞏꞏꞏꞏꞏꞏꞏꞏꞏꞏꞏꞏꞏꞏꞏꞏꞏ 이사를 ꞏꞏꞏꞏꞏꞏꞏꞏꞏꞏꞏꞏꞏꞏꞏꞏꞏꞏꞏꞏꞏꞏꞏꞏꞏꞏꞏ.

14. (만나다, 같이 하다)

좋은 사람들을 ꞏꞏꞏꞏꞏꞏꞏꞏꞏꞏꞏꞏꞏꞏꞏꞏꞏ 여행을 ꞏꞏꞏꞏꞏꞏꞏꞏꞏꞏꞏꞏꞏꞏꞏꞏꞏꞏꞏꞏꞏꞏꞏꞏ.

15. (사귀다, 배우다)

한국인 친구를 _____ 한국어를 _____.

어떻게 -게 됐어요? = How did you get to [verb]? / What made you [verb]?

    Example : (오다)

        한국에 어떻게 오게 됐어요?

16. (보다)

_____ 오디션을 _____?

17. (지원하다)

이 회사에 _____ _____?

18. (만나다)

둘은 처음에 _____ _____?

19. (시작하다)

춤은 _____ _____?

20. (알다)

이 노래는 _____ _____?

Section III - Comprehension

Complete the sentence by choosing word from each box and conjugating it with -(으)면 -게 되다.

-(으)면

| 맛있다 | 오다 | 연습하다 | 있다 | 벌다 |

-게 되다

| 타다 | 보다 | 쓰다 | 알다 | 먹다 |

21.

A: 경화 씨, 생각보다 많이 드시네요.

B: 네. ＿＿＿＿＿＿＿＿＿ 평소보다 많이 ＿＿＿＿＿＿＿＿＿.

22.

A: 많이 ＿＿＿＿＿＿＿＿＿ 많이 ＿＿＿＿＿＿＿＿＿ 것 같아요.

B: 맞아요. 아껴야 되는데.

23.

A: 무슨 일이에요?

B: 여기 ＿＿＿＿＿＿＿ ＿＿＿＿＿＿＿＿＿＿＿＿ 거예요.

24.

A: 왜 집에서 공부 안 하고 여기서 해요?

B: 집에 〰〰〰〰〰〰〰 공부 안 하고 TV 〰〰〰〰〰〰〰.

25.

A: 저는 자전거 잘 못 타요.

B: 괜찮아요. 조금만 〰〰〰〰〰〰 잘 〰〰〰〰〰〰〰〰 거예요.

Section IV - Dictation

Listen to the corresponding MP3 file. Repeat what you hear
out loud, then write it down. Each word/phrase will be said
twice.

26. Track 57

27. Track 58

Lesson 30.
Sentence Building Drill #2

Section I - Matching

Take a sentence fragment from the A Column, match it with the most appropriate fragment from column B, and write it as one sentence on the line below. .

A	B
l. 열심히 공부했는데	훨씬 덥네요.
2. 지난 주보다	보고 있어요.
3. 작년에 찍은 사진을	시험을 잘 못 봤어요.

l.

_____

2.

_____

3.

_____

	A	B
4.	친구 세 명이랑	좀 나은 것 같아요.
5.	오늘은 어제보다	혼자 잘 거예요?
6.	여기에서	여행 갔다 왔어요.

4.

_____

5.

_____

6.

_____

	A	B
7.	혼자 하는 것보다 둘이 하는 것이	아무도 모를 거예요.
8.	이렇게 더운데 밖에서	훨씬 좋은 것 같아요.
9.	제가 말 안 해서	뭐 하고 있어요?

7.

_____

8.

_____

9.

_____

	A		B
10.	바깥보다 안이	/	안 올 수도 있어요.
11.	지금 빅뱅 노래	/	훨씬 따뜻해요.
12.	효진 씨는 오늘 회사에	/	듣고 있어요.

10.

_____

11.

_____

12.

_____

Section II - Expansion Practice

Complete each sentence based on what you have learned in this lesson. Answers will vary.

13. 열 명 초대했는데, _____.

14. 올해는 작년보다 _____.

15. 지금 카페에서 _____.

16. \line 아무도 초대 안 할 거예요.

17. \line 한국어보다 훨씬 어려워요.

18. \line 일하고 있어요.

Section III - Dictation

Listen to the corresponding MP3 file. Repeat what you hear out loud, then write it down. Each word/phrase will be said twice.

19. Track 59

20. Track 60

Answer Key
for
TTMIK
Workbook
Level 4

Lesson 1

Section I - Vocabulary

1. d
2. h
3. e
4. i
5. a
6. c
7. g
8. j
9. f
10. b

Section II - Comprehension

11. 사람이 <u>많을수록</u> 좋아요.

>> The more people there are, the better it is.

12. <u>어두울수록</u> 무서워요.

>> The darker it is, the scarier it is.

13. 책이 <u>두꺼울수록</u> 무거워요.

>> The thicker the book is, the heavier it is.

14. 몸에 <u>좋을수록</u> 맛이 없어요.

>> The better it is for your health, the worse the taste is.

15. <u>배고플수록</u> 천천히 먹어야 돼요.

>> The hungrier you are, the slower you need to eat.

16. 이 노래는 <u>들을수록</u> 좋네요.

>> The more often I listen to this song, the more I like it.

Section III - Complete the Dialogue

17. A: 이렇게 비싼데, 누가 사요?

B: 사는 사람 많아요. <u>비싸면 비쌀수록</u> 잘 팔려요.

18. A: 비닐 봉투 큰 거 줄까요?

B: 네. <u>크면 클수록</u> 좋아요.

19. A: 내일 몇 시까지 올까요?

B: <u>일찍 오면 올수록</u> 좋아요.

20. A: 이 책 빨리 읽고 저 주세요.

B: 네. 책이 재미있으면 <u>재미있을수록</u> 빨리 읽을 수 있어요.

21. A: 한국어 공부는 잘 하고 있어요?

B: 네. <u>하면 할수록</u> 재미있는 것 같아요.

Section IV - Dictation

22. 바쁠수록 잠을 많이 자야 돼요.

= The busier you are, the more you need to sleep. (You need to sleep even more, especially when you are busy.)

23. 알렉스 씨는 갈수록 한국어를 잘해요.

= Alex keeps getting better at his Korean.

Lesson 2

Section I - Vocabulary

1. b
2. c
3. d
4. a
5. d
6. a
7. d

8. b

9. d

10. c

Section II - Comprehension

11. False - casual settings

12. True

13. False - 저는 안 가고 싶어요

14. False - You can put a question mark

15. True

Section III - Translation Practice

16. (저는) 집에 갈래요.

17. (저는) 혼자 할래요.

18. (저는) 쉴래요.

19. (저는) 이 영화 안 볼래요.

20. (저는) 안 먹을래요.

21. (저는) 운전할래요.

Section IV - Dictation

22. 뭐 좀 마실래요?

= Do you want something to drink?

23. 나중에 전화할래요.

= I'll call (someone) later. / I'm going to call (someone) later.

Lesson 3

Section I - Vocabulary

*from left to right

1. 선생님, 학생

2. 손님, 직원

3. 의사, 환자

4. 아빠, 엄마

5. 팬, 가수

Section II - Comprehension

6. b

7. d

8. b

9. c

10. c

Section III - Conjugation Practice

11. 할 리가 없어요.

12. 하고 있을 리가 없어요.

13. 했을 리가 없어요.

14. 할 수 있을 리가 없어요.

15. 하고 싶을 리가 없어요.

16. 해 줄 리가 없어요.

17. 해야 될 리가 없어요.

Section IV - Dictation

18. 경은 씨가 노래를 할 리가 없어요.

= There is no way that Kyeong-eun is going to sing.

19. 이상하네요. 안 될 리가 없어요.

= It's strange. There's no way that it's not going to work.

Lesson 4

Section I - Vocabulary

1. to step on; to tread on

2. to read

3. to pull, drag; to draw

4. to beg, pray

5. to cut

6. to believe, trust

7. to tie (up), bind

8. to fight, argue

9. to move

10. to wash; to rinse (out)

Section II - Comprehension

11.

a. When you are talking about something, supposing that the other person also already knows about it.

b. When both you and the other person know about something or have a common opinion about something, and you are just mentioning the fact again.

12.

c. When both you and the other person know about something, and you are just reassuring yourself by asking the question.

d. When you know about something, and you are asking yourself to confirm the fact.

e. When you don't know about something, and you are asking yourself a question, usually thinking out loud and asking the other people around at the same time.

13. d and e

Section III - Conjugation Practice

14. 우유는 거기 없지요/없죠.

15. 석진 씨가 거기 갈 리가 없지요/없죠.

16. 사무실이 너무 어두운 것 같지요/같죠?

17. 이것은 제가 들 수 있지요/있죠.

18. 그 비디오 봤지요/봤죠.

19. 일 끝나고 바로 집에 갈 거지요/거죠?

20. 이거 효진 씨가 다 해야 되지요/되죠?

21. 저도 지드래곤 콘서트 가고 싶지요/싶죠.

Section IV - Dictation

22. 그 피자는 제가 벌써 다 먹었죠. = Of course I already ate all the pizza.

23. 그럴 수도 있죠. = Yeah, that could be possible. (You and the other person both know that something is possible, and you show your agreement as the other person just mentions it.)

Lesson 5

Section I - Vocabulary

If 나 is male:

1. 할아버지

2. 할머니

3. 외할아버지

4. 외할머니

5. 큰엄마(큰어머니)

6. 큰아빠(큰아버지)

7. 고모

8. 아빠(아버지)

9. 엄마(어머니)

10. 외삼촌

11. 이모

12. 이모부

13. 사촌 형

14. 사촌 누나

15. 사촌 동생

16. 형

17. 여동생

If 나 is a female:

1. 할아버지

2. 할머니

3. 외할아버지

4. 외할머니

5. 큰엄마(큰어머니)

6. 큰아빠(큰아버지)

7. 고모

8. 아빠(아버지)

9. 엄마(어머니)

10. 외삼촌

11. 이모

12. 이모부

13. 사촌 오빠

14. 사촌 언니

15. 사촌 동생

16. 오빠

17. 여동생

Section II - Comprehension

18. If you are speaking in 반말, you can say "너."

19. If you are speaking in 존댓말, you simply say the name of the other person and add words such as -씨, -님, or a word that describes his or her position or job.

20.

a. when you are angry at someone and you don't mind fighting with that person

b. when you are translating from a foreign language and you must have a word for "you"

c. when you are writing or singing a song

d. when you are addressing your spouse (commonly used among middle-aged or older people)

e. (rare case) when you are talking about someone (who is not present in the place) in an honorific way and want to say "he" or "she"

Section III - Dictation

21. 당신 뭐가 문제야?

= What's your problem?

22. 형, 지금 어디예요?

= (Talking to your 형) Where are you right now?

Lesson 6

Section I - Vocabulary

1. exercise; workout

2. movement; move

3. operation (of a device)

4. activity

5. verb

6. animal

7. linkage; interlocking

8. behavior

9. video

10. artery

Section II - Comprehension

11. c

12. d

13. b

14. b

15. a

Section III - Dictation

16. 행동 똑바로 하세요!

= Behave yourself!

17. 리모컨이 작동이 안 돼요.

= The remote control doesn't work.

Lesson 7

Section I - Comprehension

1. d

2. c

3. a

4. c

5. b

Section II - Conjugation Practice

6. 괜찮지요.

7. 괜찮을 리가 없어요.

8. 괜찮을까요?

9. 괜찮은 것 같아요.

10. 괜찮네요.

11. 괜찮을 수도 있어요.

12. 괜찮기 전에

13. 괜찮아도

14. 괜찮은데

15. 괜찮아서

Section III - Dictation

16. 병원에 안 가도 괜찮을 것 같아요.

= I think it'll be okay even if I don't go to the hospital.

17. 석진 씨, 몸은 좀 괜찮아요?

= Seokjin, do you feel alright?

Lesson 8

Section I - Vocabulary

1. i

2. e

3. d

4. c

5. b

6. j

7. h

8. g

9. a

10. f

Section II - Comprehension

11. d

12. a

13. d

14. b

15. b

Section III - Conjugation Practice

16.

불 켜도 돼요. = You can turn the light on.

불 안 켜도 돼요. = You don't have to turn the light on.

불 켜도 돼요? = Can I turn the light on?

17.

내일 해도 돼요. = It's okay if you do it tomorrow. / You can just do it tomorrow.

내일 안 해도 돼요. = You don't have to do it tomorrow.

내일 해도 돼요? = Can I do it tomorrow?

18.

시작해도 돼요. = You can start.

시작 안 해도 돼요. = You don't have to start.

시작해도 돼요? = Can I start?

19.

이 케이크 먹어도 돼요. = You can eat this cake.

이 케이크 안 먹어도 돼요. = You don't have to eat this cake.

이 케이크 먹어도 돼요? = Can I eat this cake?

20.

이 컴퓨터 써도 돼요. = You can use this computer.

이 컴퓨터 안 써도 돼요. = You don't have to use this computer.

이 컴퓨터 써도 돼요? = Can I use this computer?

21.

오늘 쉬어도 돼요. = You can take a day off today.

오늘 안 쉬어도 돼요. = You don't have to take a day off today.

오늘 쉬어도 돼요? = Can I take a day off today?

Section IV - Dictation

22. 이 가위 써도 돼요?

= Can I use these scissors?

23. 청소 안 해도 돼요.

= You don't have to clean up. / It is okay if you don't clean up.

Lesson 9

Section I - Vocabulary

*Answers will vary. Sentences written here are examples.

1. 이야기하다

   - Definition/translation

   : to talk, to speak, to say, to tell, to have a conversation, to tell a story

   - Synonyms (in Korean)

   : 말하다

   - Sentence to help you remember

   : 무슨 이야기하고 있었어요? = What were you guys talking about?

   - Picture/drawing

   : N/A

2. 사용하다

   - Definition/translation

   : to use

- Synonyms (in Korean)

  : 쓰다, 이용하다

- Sentence to help you remember

  : 사용한 컵은 바로 씻어 주세요. = Please wash your cup right after you use it.

- Picture/drawing

  : N/A

3. 질문하다

  - Definition/translation

    : to ask a question

  - Synonyms (in Korean)

    : 물어보다, 묻다

  - Sentence to help you remember

    : 질문할 사람 있어요? = Does anyone have any questions?

  - Picture/drawing

    : N/A

4. 깜깜하다

  - Definition/translation

    : to be very dark

  - Synonyms (in Korean)

    : 캄캄하다, 어둡다

  - Sentence to help you remember

    : 깜깜한 밤에 어디 가세요? = Where are you going in this pitch-black darkness?

  - Picture/drawing

    : N/A

5. 기쁘다

  - Definition/translation

    : to be happy, to be glad

  - Synonyms (in Korean)

    : 즐겁다, 좋다, 행복하다

  - Sentence to help you remember

    : 시험에 합격해서 너무 기뻐요 = I am so happy that I passed the exam.

  - Picture/drawing

    : N/A

6. 지각하다

  - Definition/translation

    : to be late (for)

  - Synonyms (in Korean)

    : 늦다

  - Sentence to help you remember

    : 지각한 사람은 벌금 500원이에요. = A tardy person shall pay a fine of 500 won.

  - Picture/drawing

    : N/A

7. 젊다

  - Definition/translation

    : to be young

  - Synonyms (in Korean)

    : 어리다

  - Sentence to help you remember

    : 요즘 젊은 사람들이 많이 가는 곳이 어디예요? = Where do young people usually hang out these days?

  - Picture/drawing

    : N/A

8. 입장하다

  - Definition/translation

    : to enter, to go in

  - Synonyms (in Korean)

    : 들어가다, 들어오다

  - Sentence to help you remember

    : 선수들이 입장하고 있어요. = The players are entering.

- Picture/drawing

  : N/A

9. 건강하다

   - Definition/translation

     : to be healthy

   - Synonyms (in Korean)

     : 튼튼하다

   - Sentence to help you remember

     : 저희 할아버지는 아직도 정말 건강하세요.

     = My grandfather is still really healthy.

   - Picture/drawing

     : N/A

10. 교환하다

    - Definition/translation

      : to exchange, to change

    - Synonyms (in Korean)

      : 바꾸다

    - Sentence to help you remember

      : 친구들이랑 선물을 교환하고 있어요.

      = I am exchanging gifts with my friends.

    - Picture/drawing

      : N/A

Section II - Writing Practice

11. Q: 이거 제가 가져가도 돼요?

    A: (Yes) 네. (그거) 가져가도 돼요.

    A: (No) 아니요. (그거) 가져가면 안 돼요.

12. Q: 다른 채널로 돌려도 돼요?

    A: (Yes) 네. 다른 채널로 돌려도 돼요.

    A: (No) 아니요. 다른 채널로 돌리면 안 돼요.

13. Q: 이거 사용해도 돼요?

    A: (Yes) 네. (그거) 사용해도 돼요.

    A: (No) 아니요. (그거) 사용하면 안 돼요.

14. Q: 이 슬리퍼 신어도 돼요?

    A: (Yes) 네. (그 슬리퍼) 신어도 돼요.

    A: (No) 아니요. (그 슬리퍼) 신으면 안 돼요.

15. Q: 다른 사람들한테 이야기해도 돼요?

    A: (Yes) 네. 다른 사람들한테 이야기해도 돼요.

    A: (No) 아니요. 다른 사람들한테 이야기하면 안 돼요.

16. Q: 사진 찍어도 돼요?

    A: (Yes) 네. 사진 찍어도 돼요.

    A: (No) 아니요. 사진 찍으면 안 돼요.

Section III - Comprehension

17. 여기서 팔면 안 돼요?

18. 이거 만지면 안 돼요?

19. 밖에 나가면 안 돼요?

20. 창문 열면 안 돼요?

21. 이거 버리면 안 돼요?

22. 여기서 내리면 안 돼요?

23. 질문하면 안 돼요?

Section IV - Dictation

24. 내일은 절대 지각하면 안 돼요.

= You absolutely must not be late tomorrow.

25. 지금 입장하면 안 돼요?

= Am I not supposed to go in now?

Lesson 10

Section I - Vocabulary

1. 치과
2. 은행
3. 학교
4. 우체국
5. 신발가게
6. 백화점
7. 약국
8. 편의점
9. 경찰서
10. 주유소

Section II - Writing Practice

11. 편의점은 약국하고 경찰서 사이에 있어요.
12. 경찰서는 편의점하고 주유소 사이에 있어요.
13. 은행은 치과하고 학교 사이에 있어요.
14. 학교는 은행하고 우체국 사이에 있어요.
15. 우체국은 학교하고 신발 가게 사이에 있어요.

Section III - Comprehension

16. 요즘은 여섯 시에서 일곱 시 사이에 해가 떠요.

= The sun rises between 6:00 and 7:00 these days.

17. 이 가수는 한국인들 사이에서 인기가 많아요.

= This singer is popular among Koreans.

18. 책 사이에 있어서 안 보였어요.

= I couldn't see it because it was between some books.

19. 이 세 개 중에서 고르세요.

= Please choose among these three.

20. 민혁 씨, 여자들 사이에서 뭐 하세요?

= Min-hyeok, what are you doing among the girls?

21. 이 중에서 먹고 싶은 것 있어요?

= Out of these things, is there anything you want to eat?

22. 토요일하고 일요일 중에서 언제가 좋아요?

= Which day would you prefer, Saturday or Sunday?

Section IV - Dictation

23. 페이스북이 대학생들 사이에서 유행이에요.

= Facebook is all the rage among college students.

24. 꼭 이 중에서 골라야 돼요?

= Do I really have to choose among these?

Lesson 11

Section I - Vocabulary

1. anybody; doesn't matter who; anyone
2. anything; doesn't matter what
3. anywhere; any place
4. nobody; not anybody
5. nothing; not anything
6. nowhere; not any place

Section II - Fill in the Blank

7. 아무데나
8. 아무것도

9. 아무거나

10. 아무데도

11. 아무도

12. 아무나

Section III - Comprehension

13. 아무나

14. 아무나

15. 아무것도

16. 아무도

17. 아무데나/아무데도

18. 아무데도

19. 아무거나

20. 아무데나/아무데도

Section IV - Dictation

21. 아무데도 안 가고 여기 있을게요.

= I will stay here without going anywhere.

22. 아무도 만나고 싶지 않아요.

= I don't want to meet anyone.

Lesson 12

Section I - Vocabulary

1. 문제를 풀다

2. 고개를 들다

3. 한국어를 배우다

4. 가게에 들어가다

5. 운동을 시작하다

6. 이메일을 보내다

7. 상자를 열다

8. 핸드폰을 켜다

9. 거울을 보다

10. 창문을 열다

Section II - Translation Practice

11. 고개를 들어 봐요/보세요.

12. 한국어를 배워 봐요/보세요.

13. 운동을 시작해 봐요/보세요.

14. 거울을 봐 봐요/보세요.

15. 창문을 열어 봐요/보세요.

16. 문제를 풀어 봤어요?

17. 가게에 들어가 봤어요?

18. 이메일을 보내 봤어요?

19. 상자를 열어 봤어요?

20. 핸드폰을 켜 봤어요?

Section III - Conjugation Practice

21. 한국(에) 가 보고 싶어요.

22. 마카롱(을) 먹어 보고 싶어요.

23. 새로운 메뉴(를) 먹어 보고 싶어요.

24. 번지점프(를) 해 보고 싶어요.

25. 새로 나온 카메라(를) 사용해 보고 싶어요.

26. 그 노래(를) 들어 보고 싶어요.

27. 현우 씨(를) 만나 보고 싶어요.

28. 경화 씨랑 이야기해 보고 싶어요.

29. 중국어(를) 배워 보고 싶어요.

30. 새로운 일에 도전해 보고 싶어요.

Section IV - Dictation

31. 제가 먼저 해 볼게요.

= I will try doing it first. / I will give it a try first.

32. 사과랑 바나나 갈아서 만든 주스인데, 마셔 볼래요?

= This juice is made from blended apples and bananas. Do you want to try?

21. 저한테 불만 있어요?

= Do you have any complaints against me?

Lesson 13

Section I - Vocabulary, Part 1

1. anxiety; anxious
2. inconvenient; uncomfortable
3. dissatisfaction, complaint
4. wrong; unfair; unjust
5. complaint
6. distrust, mistrust
7. absence, not in attendance
8. unhappiness, misfortune
9. illegality, unlawfulness

Section II - Vocabulary, Part 2

10. 부주의(不注意): carelessness
11. 불완전(不完全): incomplete
12. 불균형(不均衡): imbalance
13. 부도덕(不道德): immorality
14. 불합격(不合格): failure; disqualification
15. 부정확(不正確): incorrect; inaccurate
16. 불이익(不利益): disadvantage
17. 불평등(不平等): inequality
18. 부적절(不適切): inappropriate
19. 부전승(不戰勝): win a game by default

Section III - Dictation

20. 제 부주의로 사고가 났어요.

= I was careless, so it caused an accident. / My carelessness caused an accident.

Lesson 14

Section I - Vocabulary

1. sometimes
2. often
3. always
4. (lit. every day) always; all the time
5. seldom; rarely
6. not at all
7. almost, nearly, all but

Section II - Checking for Understanding

N/A

8. 서점에 가다 = to go to a bookstore
9. 커피를 마시다 = to drink coffee
10. 영화를 보다 = to see a movie
11. 콘서트에 가다 = to go to a concert
12. 드라마를 보다 = to watch dramas
13. 지하철을 타다 = to take the subway
14. 야구를 하다 = to play baseball
15. 피아노를 치다 = to play the piano
16. 케이크를 만들다 = to make a cake

Section III - Reading Comprehension

17. b
18. d
19. b
20. b
21. c

Section IV - Dictation

22. 시간이 없어서 친구들을 거의 못 만나요.

= I don't have time, so I can hardly meet my friends.

23. 중국어를 맨날 공부하는데, 아직 어려워요.

= I study Chinese all the time, but it's still difficult.

Lesson 15

Section I - Vocabulary

1. 기분이 좋다

2. 놀라다

3. 힘들다

4. 기분이 나쁘다

5. 심심하다

6. 화나다

7. 졸리다

8. 슬프다

Section II - Comprehension

9. d

10. a

11. b

12. d

13. b

Section III - Writing

14. 연락

15. 일

16. 약속

17. 소식

18. 느낌

19. 옷

20. 냄새

Section IV - Dictation

21. 걱정했는데 아무렇지도 않았어요.

= I was worried, but it was okay.

22. 만드는 방법 안 배웠는데, 아무렇게나 만들어 봤어요.

= I didn't learn how to make it, and I just made it any way I wanted.

Lesson 16

Section I - Vocabulary

1. 이어폰

2. Aw, man!/Geez!

3. 휴대폰/핸드폰

4. 진짜?!

5. 대박!

6. Fighting! (Good luck!)

7. Best! / Super! / FTW!

8. 미쳤어?!

9. 세상에!

10. Selca/Self-camera/Selfie

11. 얼짱

12. Hey!

Section II - Spacing Practice

13. 가까운 역

14. 비싼 지갑

15. 추운 겨울

16. 조용한 방

17. 즐거운 토요일

18. 부지런한 사람

19. 좋은 아이디어

20. 수영 잘하는 사람

21. 피자 주문한 사람

22. 아침에 마시는 커피

23. 도서관 자주 가요?

24. 빨리 말하세요.

25. 조용히 걸으세요.

26. 어제 친구 만났어요.

27. 숙제 다 하고 왔어요.

28. 이것은 어디 있었어요?

29. 청소하고 공부했어요.

30. 저는 가끔 서점에 가요.

31. 제가 그것을 만들었어요.

32. 저는 중국어를 배우고 있어요.

Section III - Dictation

33. 방금 이상한 소리 들었어요?

= Did you hear that strange noise just now?

34. 이거 고장 난 컴퓨터 아니에요?

= Isn't this a broken computer?

Lesson 17

Section I - Vocabulary

1. e

2. k

3. g

4. m

5. j

6. i

7. l

8. c

9. f

10. a

11. h

12. d

13. b

Section II - Contraction Practice

14. 난 거실에 있을게.

15. 이게 마음에 들어요.

16. 서울엔 사람이 너무 많아요.

17. 어젠 보일러가 고장 났는데, 오늘은 세탁기가 고장 났어요.

18. 집엔 지금 누가 있어요?

19. 저것이 뭐예요?

20. 그것은 식기세척기예요.

21. 회사에는 컴퓨터가 몇 대 있어요?

22. 바다에는 언제 갔다 왔어요?

23. 여기는 에어컨이 없네요.

Section III - Dictation

24. 밤엔 동네가 조용해요.

= It is a quiet neighborhood at night.

25. 넌 뭐 먹을 거야?

= What are you going to eat?

Lesson 18

Section I - Vocabulary

1. 차갑다

   to be cold

   제일/가장 차갑다

   to be the coldest

2. 밝다

   to be bright

   제일/가장 밝다

   to be the brightest

3. 멀다

   to be far

   제일/가장 멀다

   to be the farthest

4. 뜨겁다

   to be hot

   제일/가장 뜨겁다

   to be the hottest

5. 재미있다

   to be fun

   제일/가장 재미있다

   to be the most fun

6. 얇다

   to be thin

   제일/가장 얇다

   to be the thinnest

7. 가깝다

   to be near, to be close

   제일/가장 가깝다

   to be the nearest, to be the closest

8. 두껍다

   to be thick

제일/가장 두껍다

to be the thickest

9. 재미없다

   to be boring

   제일/가장 재미없다

   to be the most boring

10. 어둡다

    to be dark

    제일/가장 어둡다

    to be the darkest

Section II - Conjugation Practice

11. 제일 차가운 아이스크림

12. 가장 밝은 방

13. 가장 먼 집

14. 제일 뜨거운 물

15. 가장 재미있는 프로그램

16. 제일 얇은 옷

17. 가장 가까운 동네

18. 가장 두꺼운 책

19. 제일 재미없는 영화

20. 제일 어두운 색깔

Section III - Writing Practice

21. 이것이 가장 쉬운 문제예요.

= This is the easiest question.

22. 어떤 원피스가 제일 예뻐요?

= Which dress is the prettiest?

23. 김태희가 제일 예쁜 배우예요.

= Kim Tae-hee is the prettiest actress.

24. 가장 가까운 화장실이 어디예요?

= Where is the nearest bathroom?

25. 이 햄버거가 가장 맛있는 햄버거예요.

= This hamburger is the tastiest hamburger.

Section IV - Dictation

26. 가장 자주 가는 커피숍이 어디예요?

= Where is the coffee shop that you visit most often?

27. 가장 재밌게 본 한국 드라마는 뭐예요?

= What is the Korean drama that you enjoyed the most? / What is your favorite K-drama?

to be greasy

덜 느끼해요.

It's less greasy.

6. 시다

to be sour

덜 셔요.

It's less sour.

7. 짜다

to be salty

덜 짜요.

It's less salty.

Lesson 19

Section I - Vocabulary

1. 달다

to be sweet/sugary

덜 달아요.

It's less sweet/sugary.

2. 쓰다

to be bitter

덜 써요.

It's less bitter.

3. 맵다

to be spicy

덜 매워요.

It's less spicy.

4. 싱겁다

to be bland

덜 싱거워요.

It's less bland.

5. 느끼하다

Section II - Writing

8. 킬리만자로 산이 에베레스트 산보다 덜 높아요.

9. 에베레스트 산이 제일/가장 높아요.

10. 킬리만자로 산이 소요산보다 더 높아요.

11. 파란색 가방이 녹색 가방보다 덜 비싸요.

12. 녹색 가방이 제일/가장 비싸요.

13. 파란색 가방이 빨간색 가방보다 더 비싸요.

14. 카이가 크리스보다 (키가) 덜 커요.

15. 크리스가 제일/가장 (키가) 커요.

16. 오세훈이 시우민보다 (키가) 더 커요.

17. 목요일이 화요일보다 덜 더워요.

18. 월요일이 제일/가장 더워요.

19. 금요일이 화요일보다 더 더워요.

Section III - Dictation

20. 어제보다는 덜 아파요.

= At least I feel less pain than I did yesterday.

21. 2편이 1편보다 덜 재미있어요.

= The sequel is not as good as the original.

Lesson 20

Section I - Matching

1. 결혼식을 위해서 오늘부터 다이어트 시작해요.

2. 어제부터 오늘까지 많은 일들이 있었어요.

3. 주말에 시간이 있으면 한번 가 보세요.

4. 언제부터 기다렸어요?

5. 지난 주부터 다음 주까지 시험 기간이에요.

6. 시간이 조금밖에 없으면 가까운 곳으로 가세요.

7. 밥 먹고 커피 마실래요?

8. 내일부터 열심히 공부할 거예요. ("내일부터 눈이 많이 내릴 거예요" is also possible.)

9. 지금 밖에 나가면 눈이 많이 내릴 거예요.

10. 내일도 어쩌면 비가 내릴지도 몰라요. ("내일도 열심히 연습할 거예요" is also possible.)

11. 석진 씨는 어떤 거 마실래요? ("석진 씨는 열심히 연습할 거예요" is also possible.)

12. 실수하지 않기 위해서 열심히 연습할 거예요.

Section II - Expansion Practice

Example answers are given below.

13. 오늘부터 한국어를 매일매일 공부할 거예요.

14. 아마 내일부터 일요일까지 비가 올 거예요.

15. 내일 시간이 있으면, 저희 집에 놀러 오세요.

16. 오후에 눈이 그칠 거예요.

17. 커피는 어디에서 마실래요?

18. 지금부터 저는 한국어로 말할 거예요.

Section IV - Dictation

19. 그제부터 비가 내리고 있는데, 내일 그칠 거예요.

= It has been raining since the day before yesterday, and it will stop tomorrow.

20. 그거 다 하고 시간이 남으면 저 좀 도와주실래요?

= If you have time after you are done with it, would you please help me?

Lesson 21

Section I - Vocabulary, Part 1

1. c
2. d
3. b
4. e
5. f
6. a

Section II - Vocabulary, Part 2

7. h
8. b
9. i
10. e
11. g

Section III - Spacing

12. 열쇠 돌려주세요.
13. 언제 돌아갈 거예요?

14. 돈 좀 빌려줄 수 있어요?

15. 한눈에 알아봤어요.

16. 들어오세요.

17. 앤디 씨는 밖에 나갔어요.

Section IV - Dictation

18. 화장을 안 하고 나가서 아무도 못 알아봤어요.

= Since I went out with no make-up on, nobody recognized me.

19. 저 다음 달에 한국으로 돌아가요.

= I am going back to Korea next month.

Lesson 22

Section I - Vocabulary

1. place; venue

2. schoolyard; playground

3. parking lot

4. scene

5. marketplace

6. farm; ranch

7. swimming pool

8. wedding hall

9. magnetic field

10. gravity field

Section II - Comprehension

11. c

12. d

13. d

14. c

15. a

Section III - Dictation

16. 이 영화에서 제일 좋아하는 장면이 뭐예요?

= What is your favorite scene from this movie?

17. 수영장에 일주일에 세 번 가요.

= I go to the swimming pool three times a week.

Lesson 23

Section I - Vocabulary

1. 직장을 얻다 = to get a job

2. 직장에 다니다/나가다 = to work, to be in paid employment

3. 직장에서 쫓겨나다/해고되다 = to be dismissed/fired from one's job

4. 직장을 구하다 = to look for a job/position

5. 직장에 적응하다 = to fit into a job

6. 직장에서 돌아오다 = to come back from work

7. 직장을 옮기다 = to move to a new workplace

8. 직장을 그만두다 = to quit a job

Section II - Conjugation Practice

9. 이렇게 = like this, in this way

10. 그렇게 = like that, in such a way

11. 저렇게 = like that (over there)

12. 이렇게 하면 = if you do it like this

13. 그렇게 하면 = if you do it in such a way

14. 저렇게 하면 = if you do it like that

Section III - Comprehension

15.

A: 좋은 직장을 얻기 위해선 어떡해야 될까요?

= In order to get a good job, what do you think I should?

B: 그러면 좋은 직장은 어떤 직장이에요?

= Then, what is a "good job"?

16.

A: 그러면 직장에서 해고될 거예요.

= If you do it like that, you will get fired.

B: 그러면 어쩌지요?

= Then, what should I do?

17.

A: 보세요. 면접에서 저러면 직장을 쉽게 구할 수 있어요.

= Look, if you do it like that at a job interview, you can easily get a job.

B: 면접이 다 저러면 저는 자신 있어요.

= If all job interviews are like that, I am sure I will do well.

Section IV - Dictation

18. 그렇게 하면 선생님한테 칭찬 받아요?

= If you do it in such a way, does your teacher give you a compliment?

19. 이거 이렇게 깨졌는데, 이제 어쩔 거예요?

= This got broken like this. What will you do with it now?

Lesson 24

Section I - Vocabulary

1. 편하다

2. 강하다

3. 깨끗하다

4. 적다

5. 많다

6. 불편하다

7. 더럽다

8. 길다

9. 짧다

10. 약하다

Section II - Fill in the Blank

11. 이 선풍기는 거실에 있는 선풍기보다 바람이 훨씬 더 약한 것 같아요.

= This fan seems to blow much weaker than the one in the living room.

12. 영화가 생각보다 훨씬 더 길었어요.

= The movie was much longer than I thought.

13. 영화관에는 사람이 주말에 훨씬 더 많아요.

= In movie theaters, there are a lot more people on the weekend.

14. 제 용돈은 언니 용돈보다 훨씬 더 적어요.

= My spending money is much less than my sister's.

15. 지난해 챔피언이 <u>훨씬 더</u> 강한 것 같아요.
= Last year's champion seems much stronger.

16. 오른쪽에 있는 의자가 높아도 <u>훨씬 덜</u> 불편해요.
= Even though the chair on the right side is high, it is much less inconvenient.

17. 지난번보다 방이 <u>훨씬 덜</u> 더럽네요.
= Wow, your room is much less dirty than last time.

18. 이 유리컵이 저 컵보다 <u>훨씬 덜</u> 깨끗해요.
= This glass is much less clean than that one.

19. 이 치마가 <u>훨씬 덜</u> 짧아서 보기 좋아요.
= Since this skirt is much longer, it looks good.

20. 이 신발이 저 신발보다 <u>훨씬 덜</u> 편한 것 같아요.
= These shoes seem much less comfortable than those shoes.

Section III - Dictation

21. 이 머리 스타일이 훨씬 더 예뻐요.
= This hair style is much prettier.

22. 이 프로그램이 훨씬 더 재미있어요.
= This program is much more interesting.

Lesson 25

Section I - Vocabulary

1. 사진이 작다 = a photo is small

2. 사진을 지우다/삭제하다 = to delete a photo

3. 사진이 잘 나오다 = a photo comes out good

4. 사진을 올리다 = to upload a photo

5. 사진을 저장하다 = to save a photo

6. 사진을 편집하다 = to edit a photo

7. 사진이 흐리게 나오다 = a photo comes out blurry

8. 사진을 찍다 = to take a photo

9. 사진을 인화하다 = to print a photo

10. 사진을 옮기다 = to transfer/load a photo

Section II - Conjugation Practice

11. 읽을 책 = book to read

12. 초대할 사람 = person to invite

13. 보낼 편지 = letter to send

14. 할 일 = work to do

15. 입을 옷 = clothes to wear

16. 볼 영화 = movie to watch

17. 외울 단어 = word to memorize

18. 공부할 언어 = language to study

19. 이야기할 사람 = person to talk (to)

20. 쓸 돈 = money to spend

Section III - Dictation

21. 내일 카페에 올 사람 있어요?
= Is there anyone who will come to the cafe tomorrow?

22. 공부할 것 가지고 2층으로 오세요.
= Bring something to study with and come up to the second floor.

Lesson 26

Section I - Vocabulary

1. 시간을 물어보다 = to ask the time
2. 시간을 지키다 = to be punctual
3. 시간이 멈추다 = time stops
4. 시간을 쏟다 = to invest/devote time
5. 시간이 걸리다 = it takes time
6. 시간을 내다 = to make time for
7. 시간이 다 되다 = time is up
8. 시간을 쓰다 = to spend time
9. 시간이 지나다/흐르다 = time passes/goes by
10. 시간이 없다 = to have no time

Section II - Comprehension

11. 어제 본 영화
12. 친구가 말한 카페
13. 어제 여기 온 사람들
14. 제일 먼저 온 사람
15. 친구한테 받은 선물

Section III - Dialogue

16. 두 권.
17. (요즘 책 읽을) 시간이 없어서.
18. 아무 때나.

Section IV - Dictation

19. 어제 먹은 메뉴가 뭐였어요?
= What was the menu item that you ate yesterday?
20. 다친 손은 다 나았어요?
= Is your wounded hand completely okay now?

Lesson 27

Section I - Vocabulary

1. 돈이 많다 = to have a lot of money, to be rich
2. 돈을 찾다 = to find money / to withdraw money
3. 돈이 부족하다 = to be short on money
4. 돈을 계산하다 = to calculate money
5. 돈을 꺼내다 = to take out money
6. 돈을 넣다 = to put money in something
7. 돈을 내다 = to pay money
8. 돈을 세다 = to count money
9. 돈이 없다 = to not have money
10. 돈을 잃어버리다 = to lose money

Section II - Tense Conjugation

11. (Present tense) 지금 비 오는 것 같아요.
(Past tense) → 새벽에 비 온 것 같아요.
(Future tense) → 내일 비 올 것 같아요.
12. (Present tense) 길이 많이 막히는 것 같아요.
(Past tense) → 길이 많이 막힌 것 같아요.
(Future tense) → 지금 가면 길이 많이 막힐 것 같아요.
13. (Present tense) 사람들이 지금 나오는 것 같아요.
(Past tense) → 사람들이 다 나온 것 같아요.
(Future tense) → 사람들이 이제 나올 것 같아요.
14. (Present tense) 수업은 매일 10시에 시작하는 것 같아요.
(Past tense) → 수업 이미 시작한 것 같아요.
(Future tense) → 수업은 10분 후에 시작할 것 같아요.

15. (Present tense) 현우 씨는 평소에 잠을 많이 자는 것 같아요.

(Past tense) → 현우 씨가 어제 잠을 많이 잔 것 같아요.

(Future tense) → 현우 씨가 오늘 피곤해서 잠을 일찍 잘 것 같아요.

Section III - Comprehension

16. 이거 뭔인 것 같아요?

17. 누가 했을 것 같아요?

18. 이게 더 좋은 것 같아요.

19. 곧 도착할 것 같아요.

20. 저 사람 한국 사람인 것 같아요.

21. 그렇게 말하면 기분 나쁠 것 같아요.

22. 제 친구가 현우 씨랑 같이 사진 찍은 것 같아요.

Section IV - Dictation

23. 저 목걸이 예쁜 것 같아요.

= I think that necklace over there is pretty.

24. 그 옷 잘 어울릴 것 같아요.

= I think those clothes will suit you well.

Lesson 28

Section I - Vocabulary

1. 얕다

2. 깊다

3. 딱딱하다

4. 부드럽다

5. 가볍다

6. 무겁다

7. 굵다

8. 가늘다

9. 느리다

10. 빠르다

Section II - Conjugation Practice

11. 가방이 훨씬 가벼워졌어요.

= [One's] bag has become much lighter.

12. 물이 훨씬 깊어졌어요.

= The water has become much deeper.

13. 걸음이 훨씬 빨라졌어요.

= [One's] walking speed has become much faster.

14. 다리가 훨씬 굵어졌어요.

= [One's] legs have become much thicker.

15. 허리가 훨씬 가늘어졌어요.

= [One's] waist has become much thinner.

16. 손바닥이 훨씬 딱딱해졌어요.

= [One's] palm has become much harder.

Section III - Writing Comprehension

17. 늦게 일어날수록 하루가 짧아져요.

= The later you get up, the shorter your day becomes.

18. 경은 씨는 갈수록 예뻐지는 것 같아요.

= I think Kyeong-eun keeps getting prettier.

19. 동영상은 길수록 지루해져요.

= The longer a video is, the more boring it gets.

20. 그 사람을 생각할수록 기분이 좋아져요.

= The more I think about him/her, the happier I get.

21. 많이 웃을수록 행복해져요.

= The more you laugh, the happier you become.

22. 이 음악은 들을수록 우울해져요. = As for this music, the more you listen to it, the more gloomy you get.

Section IV - Dictation

23. 주말이 되면 가게가 바빠져요. = When the weekend comes, the shop gets busy.

24. 제가 좋아하는 프로그램이었는데, 재미없어졌어요. = It used to be my favorite TV show, but it has become boring.

Lesson 29

Section I - Vocabulary

1. c
2. f
3. e
4. i
5. j
6. a
7. h
8. b
9. g
10. d

Section II - Conjugation Practice

11. 몸이 약해서 운동을 시작하게 됐어요.
12. 이벤트에 당첨돼서 콘서트에 가게 됐어요.

13. 직장을 옮겨서 이사를 가게 됐어요.
14. 좋은 사람들을 만나서 여행을 같이 하게 됐어요.
15. 한국인 친구를 사귀어서 한국어를 배우게 됐어요.
16. 어떻게 오디션을 보게 됐어요?
17. 이 회사에 어떻게 지원하게 됐어요?
18. 둘은 처음에 어떻게 만나게 됐어요?
19. 춤은 어떻게 시작하게 됐어요?
20. 이 노래는 어떻게 알게 됐어요?

Section III - Comprehension

21.
A: 경화 씨, 생각보다 많이 드시네요.
B: 네. 맛있으면 평소보다 많이 먹게 돼요.

22.
A: 많이 벌면 많이 쓰게 되는 것 같아요.
B: 맞아요. 아껴야 되는데.

23.
A: 무슨 일이에요?
B: 여기 오면 알게 될 거예요.

24.
A: 왜 집에서 공부 안 하고 여기서 해요?
B: 집에 있으면 공부 안 하고 TV 보게 돼요.

25.
A: 저는 자전거 잘 못 타요.
B: 괜찮아요. 조금만 연습하면 잘 타게 될 거예요.

26. 어떻게 여기서 일하게 됐어요?

= How did you come about working here?

27. 어쩌다 보니까 여기까지 오게 됐어요.

= I just happened to come this far.

Lesson 30

Section I - Matching

1. 열심히 공부했는데 시험을 잘 못 봤어요.

2. 지난 주보다 훨씬 덥네요.

3. 작년에 찍은 사진을 보고 있어요.

4. 친구 세 명이랑 여행 갔다 왔어요.

5. 오늘은 어제보다 좀 나은 것 같아요.

6. 여기에서 혼자 잘 거예요?

7. 혼자 하는 것보다 둘이 하는 것이 훨씬 좋은 것 같아요.

8. 이렇게 더운데 밖에서 뭐 하고 있어요?

9. 제가 말 안 해서 아무도 모를 거예요.

10. 바깥보다 안이 훨씬 따뜻해요.

11. 지금 빅뱅 노래 듣고 있어요.

12. 효진 씨는 오늘 회사에 안 올 수도 있어요.

Section II - Expansion Practice

Example answers are given

13. 열 명 초대했는데, 한 명 왔어요.

14. 올해는 작년보다 비가 덜 오는 것 같아요.

15. 지금 카페에서 공부하고 있어요.

16. 저는 결혼식에 제 친척들 아무도 초대 안 할 거예요.

17. 중국어가 한국어보다 훨씬 어려워요.

18. 오늘 일요일인데 일하고 있어요.

Section III - Dictation

19. 그 카페 한번 가 봤는데 사람이 너무 많았어요.

= I've been to the cafe once. There were too many people.

20. 그 과자 인기가 너무 많아서 가게에 없을 수도 있어요.

= The snack is really popular. It might not be in the store.